SEARCHING FOR MY SHANGRI LA-
TRAVELS IN S E ASIA

Also by the Author

Life with the Lions – Rugby and travel adventures in Australia following the British and Irish Lions tour of 2001

Following the Rising Sons – Rugby and travel adventures in South America and Japan following the progress of the England Rugby Team

Midlife Meanderings in SE Asia – An account of an ageing traveller's budget journeys through SE Asia

For more information and travel blogs visit
www.johnstanilandtravelwriter.com

SEARCHING FOR MY SHANGRI LA- TRAVELS IN S E ASIA

John Staniland

Copyright © 2024 John Staniland

The moral right of the author has been asserted.

Apart from any fair dealing for the purposes of research or private study, or criticism or review, as permitted under the Copyright, Designs and Patents Act 1988, this publication may only be reproduced, stored or transmitted, in any form or by any means, with the prior permission in writing of the publishers, or in the case of reprographic reproduction in accordance with the terms of licences issued by the Copyright Licensing Agency. Enquiries concerning reproduction outside those terms should be sent to the publishers.

Matador
Unit E2 Airfield Business Park,
Harrison Road, Market Harborough,
Leicestershire. LE16 7UL
Tel: 0116 2792299
Email: books@troubador.co.uk
Web: www.troubador.co.uk/matador
Twitter: @matadorbooks

ISBN 978 1805142 232

British Library Cataloguing in Publication Data.
A catalogue record for this book is available from the British Library.

Printed on FSC accredited paper
Printed and bound in Great Britain by 4edge Limited

Typeset in 12pt Minion Pro by Troubador Publishing Ltd, Leicester, UK

Matador is an imprint of Troubador Publishing Ltd

My family

Chapter 1
THAILAND REVISITED

While waiting for the overnight train to Bangkok in Nong Khai station, having just crossed over from Laos, I was sipping a contemplative coffee.

John, my recent travelling companion, was making some last-minute souvenir purchases before he flew back home to the UK. I was due in the Thai capital to meet up with my eldest daughter Marcella and her boyfriend, Brian. They were looking forward to a brief break from the British winter.

I reflected it was a new year, 2002 being just a few days old, and wondered what it would bring. 2001 had been a tumultuous year for me and the world at large. Particularly when recalling the egregious and almost incredible events of the eleventh of September in the United States of America.

That year was now done and dusted.

I had started 2001 with my mind in a maelstrom of mixed emotions. My wife and I had been drifting apart as a couple, and I could not put my finger on why this should be. Our three children were now all young adults, away studying at university, and it would appear that the empty nest syndrome was not working kindly for us. Rather than bringing us closer together, looking forwards to shared adventures without the sometimes arduous and often draining responsibilities of raising a family, it was tearing us apart.

There were no high-decibel rows and very few angry words. It was almost a quiet realisation that we were coming to the end of the road.

I finally acknowledged the elephant in the room, and not wanting the tension and the highly uncomfortable and joyless atmosphere between us to continue; I brought things to a head.

"Do you think we should split up?" I said, leaving the question hanging.

After a few moments, the sad reply, a prelude to hugs and tears, was a quiet,

"Yes."

We talked things through reasonably amicably, and we addressed practical issues over the next couple of months.

I needed to tidy up some outstanding business matters, and we readied the family home for sale.

My wife was happy to deal with the inevitable decluttering and the house sale.

"But get rid of those bloody canoes first," was a non-negotiable instruction.

I had acquired four canoes over the years that we no longer used, and luckily, I could offload them to a local scout group.

By Spring, I had decided to take a gap year out and travel throughout South East Asia. First, I would tick off a long-held dream to follow a British and Irish Lions tour to Australia.

That May, my wife and eldest daughter, gave me a lift to Heathrow. This was to be the starting point for a whistle-stop tour of India before going to the Antipodes. Virtually all my worldly possessions were in a rucksack.

What followed was a most cathartic and life-enhancing experience. My very battered and annotated Lonely Planet edition of *South East Asia on a Shoestring* helped me to follow my whims. The trip involved visiting endless fascinating places and meeting countless locals, as well as open-minded fellow travellers.

I still had many countries I wanted to visit before my planned return to Blighty in April. After spending some time in Thailand with my daughter, I would embark on a further voyage of discovery to places as yet unknown.

My itinerary was unfixed, but that was not an issue - I would make it up as I went along, as I always did; this entire episode was very much about spontaneous travel decisions.

By this time, I had taken sleeper trains frequently in Thailand and found the experience enjoyable. The accommodation was quite plain, and they maintained privacy simply by drawing a curtain across the comfortable bunk area.

The trains had relaxed restaurant cars, and it was most agreeable to have a decent if basic spicy stir-fry with a Thai beer. Enjoying this while chatting, reading or writing, and watching the twinkling lights through the windows was the order of the day.

On this occasion, John and I chatted with fellow travellers for a while before getting our heads down. Falling asleep to the regular clickety-click of the train wheels, I always enjoyed. And then waking up to see the nascent dawn light the sky over the Thai capital was awe-inspiring.

The peace and tranquillity of Laos soon became a distant memory as we entered the frantic, chaotic bustle and the hot, hazy and dust-laden world of Bangkok's famous Khao San Road. The latter was the go-to place for cheap accommodation for backpackers. As a means to an end, I found the area just about acceptable; a place to stay for a couple of cheap nights before moving on, but amazingly hordes of young backpackers seem to make the place home for weeks at a time.

We had to hang around until lunchtime to secure rooms, as the area seemed especially busy. However, once we had organised some accommodation, John had to do a few things, so I wandered off on foot to discover more hidden corners of Bangkok.

I walked along the Chao Phraya waterfront for a while. Passing the Grand Palace before discovering Bangkok's Chinatown, centred on the Yaowarat Road. It is renowned as the biggest Chinatown in the world.

The area was teeming with life, a fascinating mix of narrow sois (lanes) and busy traffic clogging the arterial roads. Wonderful old shophouses, evocative of long-gone times when the Chinese settled the area, were sitting alongside many ornate Buddhist temples.

There was a vast range of street food available, with sizzling sounds and tempting spicy aromas, making it challenging to resist. I did not; and enjoyed an excellent and very inexpensive seafood-based late lunch.

The vibrant area was a hive of industry, with thousands working hard to earn a living. Goldsmiths, jewellers, metal bashers, printers, booksellers and dressmakers were juxtaposed with mechanics, fabric stores, fancy goods outlets, moneychangers and tailors.

The Chinatown area is extensive, and I walked for miles, enjoying a fascinating stroll and absorbing the myriad of sights, sounds and odours that the district offered. I stopped for a coffee and a break for a while, then did a couple more miles before grabbing a tuk-tuk ride back to base.

After battling the rush hour traffic and taking in a few lungfuls of carbon monoxide, sulphur dioxide and other common pollutants on the hot, sweaty twenty-minute ride back, I arrived at our temporary home. I then showered and changed in readiness to meet up with John and celebrate the last night of his trip.

After a pleasantly civilised meal and a few drinks in the local Khao San Road area, we retired relatively early, as John had an early departure.

I checked out mid-morning and headed off to explore more random parts of the fascinating city. Marcella had insisted that she would treat me to a night in more salubrious accommodation than I had been used to. To be fair, I was more than happy with my usual standard of place, but she insisted.

They, therefore, booked me into the Tower Inn on central Silom Road. The place had an open-air rooftop pool and a gym, so it would make an agreeable change to have such facilities at my disposal.

I booked in and stashed my bag before walking the down the

long Silom Road and finding myself in the lively and cosmopolitan Sukhumvit Road area.

The place was thrumming with high-energy activity, a cacophony of noise and general commotion. Throngs of people, noxious traffic fumes, market traders and upmarket shopping malls, combined with roads full of suicidal motorcyclists and tuk-tuk drivers. The street food aromas were wonderful, though. All these sights, sounds and smells were readily associated with downtown Bangkok. It was a heady mix, and I wandered around for a while, taking it all in before walking back to make our pre-arranged meeting.

Cella and Brian were looking forward to a week's holiday in Thailand. They were starting with a brief taste of full-on Bangkok - the temples and markets, river trips, restaurants and renowned nightlife. After a couple of high-octane days, it would be beach time. We were planning for a few days' stay down south on one of the islands, the exact location of which was still to be determined.

Once we had met up and relaxed with a cocktail or two, they outlined their plans for the next couple of days. It sounded pretty hectic.

"I'll just dip in and out if that's ok with you?" I said.

They were buzzing with excitement, jet lag and a couple of potent Mai Thais. They told me they were keen to go to the newly opened and extravagantly and expensively fitted out Ministry of Sound club later. I had recently read about this flagship opening in the *Bangkok Post*.

It was still early, so we ventured out into the sultry Bangkok evening. We were aiming to find somewhere for a couple more pre-dinner drinks and then an authentic and non-touristy Thai restaurant for dinner. Having escaped the dull, cold and dreary UK winter, they were keen to have a complete and rapid immersion into the SE Asian experience. From my point of view, it was terrific to catch up with news from home after being on the road for nearly eight months. Also to feed off their excitement at being at an exhilarating holiday destination halfway across the world.

After a superb 'pushing the boat out meal', we ventured off to find the Ministry of Sound. The entry system was strange in that admission was free, but they kept a tab of drinks purchased, the bill being settled before leaving. I could thus check the place out for myself and experience the incredible sound system where you could literally 'feel the noise.' Standing in awe watching the spectacular light show for a while, sipping a beer and watching the 'beautiful people' dancing was fun. After a while, I excused myself and left them to it.

I found a vibrant bar advertising live music and where a talented band of older musos were playing a heady mix of rock and blues covers. 'Route 66' was more like it for me.

I spent a great evening meeting some like-minded travellers to share drinks and stories with before opting for a hairy motorcycle taxi ride back. The alcohol intake probably made me feel quite fatalistic about the trip.

The following day, after enjoying an excellent buffet breakfast, something I was not used to, I lay by the pool. Knowing it would be a while before the partying duo emerged, I settled down with my book. By noon, with still no appearance, I made good use of the hotel's gym and then completed a few energetic lengths of the pool.

By 2 pm, the miscreants appeared, and we headed out to undertake a whistle-stop tour - given our limited time availability - and explore the Thai capital. We took in the green oasis of Lumpini Park, which was close to the hotel. We then strolled along the banks of the Chao Praya River and visited the Grand Palace. A longtail boat ride allowed us to see the city from the river. We saw the spectacular riverside Wat Arun and found some tranquil and leafy narrow sois on the quieter side of the river.

This latter area was a world apart from the noisy Bangkok traffic, the hordes of people, and the oppressive heat. The dark green trees curved over to provide a welcoming, cooling canopy. The lack of human and vehicular traffic gave the area a peaceful air. To which an abundance of chirruping birds and buzzing insects provided an enchanting and sonorous backdrop.

I sat on the terrace of a friendly little bar restaurant with a drink and a snack whilst Cella had her hair cut at the salon next door. Brian accompanied her, taking a professional interest as he was a hairstylist back home.

It was a brief sojourn in Bangkok, as we had to get to the station to catch the overnight sleeper down to Surat Thani. After, we would head westwards by bus across the narrow neck of land to Krabi and decide which island paradise to honour with a visit.

The 6 pm train overnight to Surat Thani took twelve hours. From there, it was an early morning trip across to Krabi, the gateway to many of the beautiful islands of the Andaman Sea.

On a whim, and partly because a young American guy gave me a 200-baht boat ticket, we headed for Ko Lanta.

Unfortunately, the vessel developed some engine problems that the crew could not fix readily. So we bobbed around on the ocean for twenty minutes until a replacement vessel could draw alongside. Then, tentatively, as there was a fair swell, we stepped onto the rescue boat.

I Chatted to a young Australian woman on the new sizeable longtail vessel. She strongly recommended a newly developed stretch of bars and bungalows on Long Beach.

"It's secluded and quite relaxing, but with a bit of bar action. I stayed a few weeks ago, and the different places offer different vibes in terms of music and food. It is very inexpensive as well. You'll love it. It's great, really great." she gushed.

The Aussie girl's description sounded ideal, so we agreed we would check it out.

Long Beach turned out to be as idyllic as we'd been told in terms of it being a fantastic 4km stretch of perfect sandy beach. Backed by swaying palms with warm turquoise waters lapping gently at the shoreline, it was truly beautiful. Just what the doctor ordered for a relaxing beach break.

The accommodation was simple bamboo and timber-built, self-contained chalets. These featured a double bedroom (complete with mosquito net), a bathroom with shower and a veranda with a hammock and chairs and a table facing the ocean.

The business model was for a set of a dozen bungalows, pitched at slightly different markets. Their own palapa-roofed bar, snack bar or restaurant, doubled up as reception. There were probably about a dozen of these small independent enterprises spread along the beach. It was just what we wanted for a relaxing few days.

I took a modestly priced place for 250 baht a night (about a fiver). The other two plumped for a slightly posher and perhaps more spacious version at the establishment next door for around 400 baht.

We still had a couple of hours of daylight to get ourselves sorted out and explore the beach a bit more. Swimming in the warm and inviting Andaman Sea was wonderful. Then at dusk, having showered off the sand and salt, we met up at my bar for a sundowner and watched the moon dancing on the water. It was mesmerising, particularly for two people freshly arrived from the English winter.

After a couple of aperitifs, as my place only offered simple snacks, we moved on to find a restaurant. We soon came across a larger, more sophisticated eatery that already had a few early diners in place. This created a pleasant but very chilled-out atmosphere. We ordered beautifully creamy, spicy green curries, washing them down with ice-cold beers.

Then we explored the different options along the beach. Some bars catered to party animals with loud rock music. Others offered ambient vibes or had a hippy feel. There were more than a few offering Bob Marley's reggae on the sound system.

With the neon lights, amplified music, open fire pits, young Thais performing fire-eating demonstrations and dancing with swinging poi or fireballs, it made for an exciting feast for the senses.

Acrobatically spinning and twisting skilfully whilst juggling flaming torches, the local entertainers put on quite a show. Later in the evening, backpackers fortified by the plastic buckets of cocktails they had been glugging had gained enough Dutch courage to take to the floor and attempt to skip burning ropes. Or else get involved with other forms of pyrotechnics. Not something to be recommended.

After a while, I left Cella and Brian at a wilder party bar whilst I backtracked to a place I had spotted earlier. This offered some comfortable seating, pleasant ambient sounds, and, importantly for me, an area where the lighting was good enough to read. For an hour, I settled down with my book.

I rose early the next day to enjoy a long walk along the beach in the relatively cool morning air. A luxury resort was under construction at the end of Long Beach. The upmarket accommodation would inevitably be a self-contained resort facility offering a range of high-end accommodations. There would also be swimming pools, spas, tennis courts, restaurants and an army of uniformed flunkies to cater for every whim. They would employ security guards to keep the hoi polloi and backpackers at a safe distance. The luxury market was going to be the way forward for the Thai hospitality industry. They would probably price me out of the market on subsequent visits to this beautiful country.

I walked on further to see miles of beautiful empty sand and ocean backed by dense acreages of verdant jungle.

I doubled back and enjoyed a fresh fruit and coffee breakfast at one of the earlier opening places on Long Beach. It was excellent preparation for a day of doing not a lot in the sunshine.

We enjoyably spent the next couple of days swimming, sunbathing, eating, drinking, relaxing, chatting and reading. A most acceptable antidote to travelling for a while.

We hired motorbikes one day, however, and explored the island. The ubiquitous 125cc machines were good fun, but the roads and tracks were abysmal and severely rutted. It was incredibly straightforward to come a cropper if you did not have your wits about you. The sight of several bandaged and limping backpackers attested to this. It brought about a painful and expensive end to the SE Asia adventures for more than a few travellers.

However, the motorbikes were great for seeing the island and interacting with the locals. Young, smiling children would cheer and wave as we rode through their small villages. We needed to steer carefully around a variety of livestock and the crowds of locals attending the markets.

We passed palm and coconut groves and rubber plantations in the countryside, the latter with sheets of raw latex, like so many huge bathmats drying in the sun. There were orchards and stands of fruit trees and vendors at the roadside selling piles of succulent oranges, plantains and coconuts.

We continued up and down the hills of the interior, negotiating the road hazards carefully. Later, we stopped at a lookout point advertising a 'Very Nice View'. They would not have fallen foul of trade description legislation for such signage.

We were up high, looking east over the sea to where a collection of a dozen or more craggy, vertiginous, silvery limestone outcrops clad in dark green foliage shimmered in the heat haze above the turquoise waters. We could see the odd brightly painted longtails making their way between the islets. The putt-putt of throbbing engine sounds drifted up on the breeze, as warm and gentle as a kitten's sneeze. Many small stationary fishing boats bobbed about. Their crews were intent on harvesting the piscatorial bounty for that night's dinner.

"Isn't it wonderful? Beautiful!" cried Marcella.

We both nodded in agreement. It was indeed a feast for the eyes.

After 'Very Nice View', we descended via a steep and curving trail into the self-deprecatingly named 'Nice Beach'. Here we enjoyed an excellent grilled king prawn lunch before exploring the little village.

On a whim, we all booked up for a four-island snorkelling tour the next day at a small beachside tourist operation. Snorkelling some of the prolific reefs would undoubtedly be something with which to look forward.

Then we headed home via Saladan, the port area, and a bustling settlement with lots of delightful wooden houses built out over the water. We parked up and checked the place out a little, and I bumped into someone I knew from back home, as I often seemed to do on my travels.

Back in Long Beach for the evening, we ended up at Reggae Bar. This was a very bohemian place with lots of art trouve and cool furniture made of bits of scrap iron and driftwood. Seating platforms with scores of multicoloured cushions and blankets and hammocks were set around an open fire pit. It had a very relaxed feel and, of course, plenty of Marley plus Dylan and Hendrix playing. There were also plenty of Singha and Chang beers and the ubiquitous Thai whisky available. The staff wore Che Guevara tee-shirts, and a number sported impressive dreadlocks to complete the theme.

Early the next morning, as promised, an agricultural-smelling songthaew turned up for us. Rattling along for a few miles, we pulled up at to a small bay up the coast where a colourful longtail boat was floating offshore in the gentle surf. We were soon off, zooming over the ocean thanks to the vast seven-litre Chrysler car engine attached to a glorified food mixer.

After picking up four young Canadians on Nice Beach, we headed on in a south-easterly direction for an hour. Anchoring off a small green-clad island with a fringing reef, we prepared to do some snorkelling. We were soon in a warm, tranquil underwater world. Vast shoals of multi-hued fishes, swaying sea anemones, fronds of delicate seaweed and exotically shaped and strikingly coloured coral offered a superb sight. The entire party got stung by tiny jellyfish, but as this was only of the order of a nettle sting, it did not cause any undue stress. We were not in deadly box jellyfish territory here.

The skipper called us back after twenty minutes of snorkelling. We then motored on to a second islet. The new reef was an even better location, with a more incredible selection of both fish and coral.

They then took us to Ko Muk while eating our fresh fruit and vegetable rice packed lunch, which was provided as part of the trip. This island featured the renowned Emerald Cove, 'Morokot' in Thai. We anchored just off what we could make out as the opening to the dark cavern.

One of the young Thais acted as a guide, encouraging us to swim up to the cave's entrance. The dense foliage on the sheer limestone above had grown over to form a canopy and block out much of the sunlight. We swam slowly and silently in the eerie darkness for some eighty metres, taking care to avoid bashing into the rocky sides as the tunnel narrowed. Finally, we emerged into a magical sunlit cove of soft sand. This was a beautiful hidden beach utterly open to the sky where the roof of the cave had fallen in many years before. It was an enchanting place, and we stayed for a while, relaxing on our private secluded beach, listening to the gentle waves breaking on the shoreline. A piece of Thai heaven.

After a couple of more days of Thai hedonism on beautiful Ko Lanta, it was time to move on. Cella and Brian going back to cold and gloomy Blighty and me to pastures new, still to be decided.

*

With the other two heading up by train to Bangkok from Trang, I took a boat over to Ko Phi Phi. I planned to go on to Phuket and perhaps see whether I could get a crewing job on a sailing vessel going down south somehow. Maybe unlikely, but I wouldn't know if I didn't try.

Phi Phi was like I had left it in October, just a little busier and a little pricier. There was a lot of pressure on the charming tiny island to cope with the tourist numbers they received. Water supply, litter and refuse, and sanitation were among the most pressing problems the authorities had to deal with.

I picked up a day-old copy of the *Bangkok Post* and read an article on Phi Phi. The piece argued the island needed to close to tourists for an extended period until the authorities could resolve the many issues. With all the considerable vested commercial interests involved, this was as unlikely to happen as turkeys voting for Christmas.

Tragically, the island, a few years later, in the December 2004 tsunami, suffered incredibly. Reports were that 4,000 lost their lives to that massive Indian Ocean tidal wave, and it destroyed the island's infrastructure. One survivor described the aftermath as being as;

"It was as if the island had been picked up by an angry giant and thrown down again."

I only stayed in town for 24 hours, reacquainting myself with my old haunts and even meeting up with some locals and travellers I had met a few months earlier.

Once in Phuket, I took a songthaew to the brash beach resort of Patong and found a modest new guesthouse close to the beach. It was an agreeable enough beach but spoiled for me by the constant loud droning of powerful jet skis that plagued the busy shoreline and beyond.

Patong was throbbing from dusk to dawn with all the usual sizeable Thai resort activities, so I had a good mooch around, a reasonable meal, and a couple of beers. I also unearthed an excellent backstreet live band place with an ex-pat band playing for my evening's entertainment.

I planned to see if I could bum a lift on a boat down to Malaysia or Indonesia. The next day, I hired a motorcycle and headed off to check out various marinas and yacht havens. Perhaps I might be lucky and someone would need a general dogsbody to help on a voyage down south.

Unfortunately, I drew a blank with this plan - it was quickly apparent that there were considerably more job seekers than vacancies. More hopeful crew members than desperate skippers.

I enjoyed motorbiking around though; the roads were a lot better maintained than in Ko Lanta. It was a great way to explore Phuket and discover some of the island's hidden charms, of which there were more than a few. Away from the main resort areas, Phuket offered some picturesque and unspoiled bays and beaches.

I decided to head south anyway, even if it meant paying for the privilege. The following day found me on an early morning boat sailing over the increasingly familiar but no less impressive Andaman Sea, bound for Krabi.

The longtail boat beached (literally) at Ao Nang. Disembarking without getting soaked was, therefore, tricky. I was familiar with Ao

Nang, around the corner from the fabulous Railay Beach and just a quick ride from Krabi town.

I took the brief boat ride over to Railay from Krabi for another look at this exceptional place.

Railay Beach is one of the standout places in Thailand, and that is saying something. I initially thought the place was an island. But it is a peninsula hemmed in by thickly forested limestone peaks, making it completely inaccessible by road.

The main beaches, Railay West, Railay East and the fabulous Phra Nang are picture-perfect. Curves of soft yellow-white sand caressed by a gentle bluish-green sea with craggy limestone islets. These colossal peaks, flecked with deep green foliage, were like sentinels lying a little offshore.

Phra Nang is a very strong contender for the best beach I have ever seen, along with Whitehaven Beach in Australia's Whit Sunday Islands. Exquisite - and the reason I took I took a diversionary boat trip out for another look.

The tall, almost vertical limestone crags flanking the bay made the place a mecca for rock climbers. Watching the young Thais, many in just a pair of shorts and no footwear, racing up the rock faces like demented monkeys, was always quite a spectacle.

And, speaking of simians, troupes of sea monkeys do actually live in the area. They have adapted their lifestyles most intelligently to become fishers. Ingeniously, they use small rocks to smash open clams, mussels and limpets to access the succulent flesh.

The songthaew connection from Ao Nang dropped me conveniently at Krabi bus station. Here, I quickly established that there was shortly a bus going to Satun on the Thai-Malaysian border.

It was a four-and-a-half-hour trip, which wasn't a brilliant prospect. When I saw the state of the battered old vehicle I would travel on, it inclined me to think again about taking the trip. But, having a second look, it was not excessively full, and I could secure one of the more spacious backseat slots. The comfortable berth enabled me to pass a reasonably pleasant trip. Spending the time dozing, reading, daydreaming, and enjoying looking out at the passing countryside was more than acceptable.

I found a room, for a reasonable rate, in a large, crumbling old hotel of some charm and character and set out to explore the attractive and sizeable town. I had a pleasant stroll around the place before having supper at a smart restaurant called Time. After a couple of nightcaps, I headed for bed at about 10 pm.

Up early, I was on the move again, taking a motorbike taxi out to the port to secure a ticket for the ferry across to the Malaysian island of Langkawi.

Chapter 2

LANGKAWI AND PENANG

I had given myself plenty of time to organise the formalities, and it was not busy. Just one chap was in front of me in the queue. However, it appeared that this bloke had an insurmountable problem that the staff could not resolve. It turned out the two surly and completely uninterested staff behind the shabby counter were patently ignoring his pleas. They just carried on moving bits of paper around the office at a glacial pace. The female staff member huffed and sighed and appeared to have the world's troubles on her shoulders, but would not deign to deal with an actual customer. Superior in status and attitude, the male felt himself above doing any work at all, merely intent on practising his snarl. He looked like a villain in a Bond movie if Bond villains cleaned out their fingernails with a pencil rather than a fearsome-looking knife.

Eventually, I got to the desk as the previous customer finally received his tickets. I approached the official and politely asked for a travel voucher. He dismissively and soundlessly pointed to the female who had now moved to a position behind a small hatch further along the counter. She begrudgingly processed a ticket, and I handed her a 500 baht banknote for the 180 baht fare. The piece of paper was first passed to the male official, who had to give it some form of senior approval. Having done so, he handed it to me, at the same time dismissing me with a wave and, speaking for the first time, grunted,

"Ferry there."

I politely pointed out the small matter of my 320 baht change.

He huffed and puffed, sighed and snarled, and I sensed I was being categorised as an awkward customer, a troublemaker. His face reddened, and he became more and more animated with exaggerated facial contortions and frantic arm-waving. There was no change float, and he had to dig into his pockets to find the notes from his wallet. Finally, he gave me what I was owed, and he aggressively waved me away. The clock on the wall behind him showed 8 am, the departure time.

I still had passport control to get through. The customs office a few yards along had a sign above a small window saying 'Queue Here' and another on the counter saying 'Closed'.

I looked around, becoming anxious that I would miss the boat. Spotting a young man in the ferry company livery, he told me the ferry was not leaving for half an hour.

I sat on a chair outside the passport counter and waited. Eventually, a tall, skinny, lugubrious young man with an officious manner appeared from a back office. He strutted about self-importantly and looked around condescendingly. Then hacking theatrically, gobbed impressively, and lit up a cigarette. Lingering over his smoke for ten minutes, he then went back into the office, reappearing at the hatch. With a sigh, he slammed open the glass-fronted hatch and gestured impatiently for my passport.

As I had entered Thailand on at least four occasions since September, there were stamps everywhere. He showed his obvious annoyance at not being able to locate the proper visa stamp quickly enough. After flicking through the pages for several minutes, he found the relevant mark. He smashed it into oblivion with his hand stamp before flinging it back in my direction.

"Thank you, sir," I said, smiling politely.

At last, I was underway, and the trip of just over an hour on the modern speedy vessel went without a hitch. I spent it relaxing on deck enjoying the sunshine, which was pleasantly tempered by the sea breeze.

Then, before long, I was completing lengthy immigration forms to prepare for disembarking at Langkawi's port, Kuah.

In due course, I handed the immigration forms and my passport to another bumptious, supercilious government official. He regarded my passport like something repulsive he had found on the bottom of his shoe. It was a good day for bureaucratic arseholes.

Admittedly, it was no longer a pristine document, inadvertently having got a soaking when I was whitewater rafting in the Ping River in Northern Thailand some months back. I thought it had dried out pretty well, all things considered.

Gingerly holding the offending article between forefinger and thumb, he opened it, closed it, turned it around, turned it over, sighed melodramatically, and finally put it down. He then looked at me contemptuously, like a Victorian schoolmaster might have regarded a third former who had blotted his copybook.

He stared at me, and I glared back, holding his gaze. I had had more than enough petty officials for a while.

"Passport is not good," he finally offered, with his meanest glare.

I carried on, staring silently and intently. *Fornicating onanist*, I thought to myself.

The bumptious bureaucrat held up the offending article to show how crumpled it was. Making a grand display of flattening it out before he finally applied his coup de grâce stamp, all the time mumbling to himself.

"Why is it like that? Not good!"

Because it's been for half a day's fucking swim, mate. I wanted to yell but didn't.

He finally handed the passport back and disdainfully waved me through. I allowed a beatific smile to play across my face and said,

"Thank you, sir."

With landscaped gardens, water features and pleasing patio areas in front of the harbour, the modern port buildings formed part of an impressive gateway to Langkawi's capital town of Kuah. A spectacularly massive statue of a ruddy-brown eagle (the literal translation of Langkawi being eagle) cast its beady eye over the waters.

The town centre appeared to be only a mile or so away, so I eschewed the offers of the many taxi drivers hovering around. I strode off purposefully to find some accommodation.

On the edge of the central business district, I came across a suitable contender. The slightly shabby and down-at-heel business hotel was reasonably cheap. It offered an excellent double room with a certain charm and a considerable full-height shuttered window facing the city.

I was soon exploring the modern town that was Kuah. It appeared to be a significant duty-free shopping mecca, with scores of high-end luxury goods retail outlets. These held no interest for me but were a big draw for many visitors. The place did not have any semblance of a soul, though, and I knew I would not be staying long.

It was still my intention to secure a passage crewing on some form of sailing or powerboat. It was an idea that had captured my imagination, and I was keen to see if Langkawi could come up trumps.

I hired a motorbike to enable me to explore the island and check out marinas and yacht clubs. Whether I would be successful was not an issue. Getting a motorbike was an excellent way of covering the entire island quickly and finding out something about its DNA.

I started by visiting the Royal Langkawi Yacht Club. This I quickly found to be a most acceptable place to relax with an ice-cold beer in the hot sunshine for half an hour. The open-fronted, expensively fitted bar was a glorious spot to watch the gleaming white mono-hulls and catamarans bobbing up and down at their moorings in the stiff breeze.

It would have been nice to be sailing off on one of those beautiful vessels, but it was not looking destined to be. The pleasant man at the bar had told me most clearly, nobody was looking for crew members.

I remounted my Honda and headed off westwards towards Cenang Beach. En route, I came across Porto Malai, which was the home base for Star Cruises. A magnificent four-masted clipper, the *Star Flyer*, was lying at berth. It was well over a hundred metres long. Looking gleamingly exquisite in the bright sunshine, I approached to have a closer look. The majesty of the venerable old sailing vessel was quite something to behold.

"She's a real beaut, isn't she?" an overweight, middle-aged Aussie offered.

He had just come down the gangplank accompanied by his elegant, slim wife and looked as proud as punch to be associated with such a fantastic mode of transport.

"We just came down from Phuket," he continued. "Bit of drama last night, though. The sail on the central mast is the largest in the world. Completely bloody blew out in the middle of the night. Went like a bloody thunderclap. It was very gusty, I suppose. Talk about 'all hands on deck'. They were running around like blue-arsed flies and got it down with a bit of a struggle. And then they were all out with their sewing kits to do a repair job. I watched it all. Fascinating."

We chatted a little longer, and I learned they were cruising up to northern Thailand for a few days. A little enviously, I fired up my bike and said my goodbyes, wishing them both an enjoyable trip.

I decided the idea of getting a crewing job was fast becoming a non-starter.

I rode to Cenang, a pleasant enough beach resort with an impressive arc of sand and green islets offshore sprouting out of the turquoise Andaman Sea. There was a strip of tourist-orientated bars, restaurants, and shops. I followed the coast a while longer, passing innumerable upmarket resort hotels and villas. Finally, I cut inland, heading back to base by going cross-country. In the middle of the island, it was a different world of undulating hills, grazing water buffalo, rice paddies and palm groves.

The following morning, I took the motorbike out to explore other parts of the island. Voyage of discovery over, I returned it to the rental office and caught the 2 pm fast ferry for Penang.

*

British colonial influence in Penang was clear as we berthed at Georgetown, the island's handsome capital. We docked at a solidly constructed former naval dockyard of some antiquity rather than a modern ferry terminal. I emerged from a confusing succession of tunnels and passages into the bright sunlight to be confronted by the striking white structure that was Fort Cornwallis. This magnificent edifice is a standing testament to the British rule of the region some 225 years before. I saw a fine clock tower dedicated to Queen Victoria's Golden Jubilee standing proudly in its neat gardens. Standing for a while, as I was in no great hurry, I admired the historic edifice.

I hefted my rucksack onto my shoulder and walked down Lebuk Light, or Light Street. This thoroughfare was named after Captain Francis Light, who secured Penang for the East India Company in 1786. The place exuded history, and I was looking forward to exploring what seemed already to be a fascinating city. Particularly when compared to the soulless Langkawi I had just left behind.

I was aiming for Lebuk Chulia, where I had learned I might find a cluster of budget hotels, and I should be able to secure some accommodation.

A little way from the port, though, I passed by one of the most famous colonial hotels in the world. Perched proudly on the shoreline, the Eastern and Oriental, or E&O, for those in the know, stood bright, white and magnificent. This superb colonial building, dating from 1885, provoked me to stop and stare for a few moments to take in its beauty. I felt a slight twinge of envy that my budget would not run to a few nights there.

Reluctantly, I had to walk on. Then, inadvertently and accidentally, I suddenly found myself in a buzzing, raucous district with a heady mix of sounds, sights and fragrances battling for supremacy. Incense, joss sticks and a range of fragrant spices fought for olfactory attention with curries, outdoor tandoori ovens and sweet-smelling loaves of bread. Stallholders stylishly displayed beautiful, brightly coloured bolts of fabrics on trestles. Other vendors set pyramids of shiny fruits and vegetables out for sale. Jangling Indian pop clashed with traffic noise, car horns and the general hubbub of commerce. I was in the enthralling 'Little India' area.

In the nineteenth century, the British colonial rulers encouraged Indians to settle and work on the plantations or major building projects like the new railway infrastructure. They thrived, and their continued presence in large numbers adds significantly to the vibrant cultural mix of Georgetown.

I reached Lebuk Chulia, carefully avoiding being knocked over by one of the many rickshaws and trishaws. In front of me, the splendour of an elaborately ornate Chinese temple featuring multi-hued dragons and paintings of fearsome bearded warriors caught my eye. Just beyond, I could see the magnificent Kapitan Keling Mosque, a superb wedding cake of a building. The mosque with a roof of orange pantiles topped with black and golden onion domes glinting in the sun looked exquisite.

To my right, down Lebuk Queen, running parallel to Penang Street and a part of Little India, was the splendid Sri Mariamman Temple.

The architects had adorned this famous place of worship with ornate carvings and sculptures of brightly coloured Hindu deities. These included elephant-headed gods, corpulent Buddha-like figures and heavily bosomed female goddesses.

The whole place was a dramatic and intense feast for the eyes.

Further down the street, I quickly found eminently suitable accommodation. I had located a lovely, sizeable, balconied, first-floor room in an authentic old wooden shophouse. A large double bed made up with crisp white linen, polished bare wood floors with colourful rugs, full-height shuttered windows, and tall ceilings made it a charming place to call home for a few days.

Excited by what I had seen of Georgetown in my first half-hour, I was keen just to dump my rucksack. I was soon back out onto the vibrant streets and continue my explorations. Relieved of baggage, I had a spring in my step and pondered which way to go. It was a kid in a sweet shop moment.

I homed in on Chinatown, the largest and best-preserved in the region. The Chinese community plays an integral part in the Penang business and social world, with many people of Chinese extraction holding senior positions in the city and state government structures. Twenty Chinese temples and clan houses (rather like trade associations) spread throughout a small network of streets, all looking impressive. These quite spectacular buildings had spread eagle roofs and elaborately detailed frescoes, friezes and bas-reliefs.

Along Lebuk Leith is the Cheong Fatt Tze Mansion, an acclaimed masterpiece of Chinese architecture. Primarily built in a Chinese Imperial style but with nods towards British Victoriana, it boasted intricate wrought ironwork features and beautiful imported porcelain floor tiling from Stoke-on-Trent. Painted an indigo blue, the 38-room property, was originally built for the eponymous Fatt Tze, a highly successful merchant in the late nineteenth century. The building is commonly and affectionately known as the Blue Mansion. It was now a UNESCO-protected building operating as a high-end boutique hotel.

I came across the mansion as dusk was falling and they had just switched the floodlights on, which showed the magnificent structure dramatically illuminated to maximum effect.

Opposite the mansion was a row of tastefully refurbished shophouses. One was an upmarket Indian restaurant and another an elegant pub bistro. I promised myself I would check them out later.

I could see that Georgetown was bursting with opportunities for some wonderful exploration. Such a wealth of colonial heritage sites, a vibrant mix of cultures, ethnicities, religions and languages, with the inhabitants rubbing along well enough together with no undue issues. I was enjoying being in the mix. The place was undoubtedly a unique blend of east and west, an authentic Pearl of the Orient, an appellation it shares with several other worthy contenders.

By now, I was ready for something to eat and, as I had somehow re-entered Little India, opted for some excellent street food advertised as 'Tandoori Set'. Lots of little basic restaurants with a few rickety tables and chairs set on the pavement offered this meal option, and I chose one being run by a smiling and welcoming young man.

"We are the best, sir! You will enjoy, I promise!" he told me enthusiastically, and it inclined me to believe him.

They had huge charcoal-fired tandoors or clay ovens set up for the naans and the skewers of tandoori marinated chicken. An assistant slapped the naan dough in a skilful and well-practised manner onto the sides of the tandoor, where it stuck until baked. The chefs then hung skewers of meat around the second red-hot oven. A large soot-blackened pot of spiced lentils was bubbling on the stove. Tandoori chicken, naan and dhal - just like home, I thought to myself, the difference being this superb offering could not be fresher and was available at a tenth of the price.

As it was peak dinner time by now, all these tiny restaurants seemed to do very well, the freshness, quality and rapid turnover ensuring both excellence and value.

The following morning, after opening my bedroom shutters on to a clear sunny day, I continued my explorations of Georgetown on foot. After a relaxed coffee at a convenient street stall opposite my guesthouse, I ventured further afield, just following my nose, drinking in the incredible atmosphere. The place undeniably offered a sensory explosion.

I soon came across the Eastern and Oriental, a little unexpectedly as I had approached from a different angle, but this time, I paid a closer visit, unencumbered by my rucksack.

I entered the reception area, confidently striding past liveried staff in knee-length khaki shorts and long white socks and topped with topis.

Acting like I owned the place, I could check out the lounges, the bars, the conservatories, and the gardens. Stylish, well-travelled Europeans of advanced years were taking morning coffee or perhaps enjoying a small pre-prandial snifter.

Purely coincidentally, I learned they had only recently reopened the hotel after a substantial refurbishment programme, so I saw the place at its absolute and excellent best. It honoured me to be walking in the footsteps of such luminaries as Noel Coward, Douglas Fairbanks, Somerset Maugham, Charles Chaplin, Rudyard Kipling and Chinese leader Sun Yat-sen.

The Sarkies, brothers of Armenian descent, who later added Raffles in Singapore and The Strand in Rangoon to their impressive collection of prestigious hotels built the E&O.

I reluctantly took my leave, having undertaken a thorough exploration, with a nod of the head to the immaculately dressed doorman and carried on with my circuitous perambulations.

I later stumbled across a delightful and tranquil little courtyard area off Beach Road. A modestly sized Chinese temple with bright scarlet and blue dragons on the roof sat in the middle of twenty or more neat shophouses. The majority had attractive, apparently original, wooden shutters at the first-floor windows.

Close by on Cannon Square, I found the highly ornamented and colourful Khoo Kongsi, reputed to be the grandest clan house in all of Penang. The building was a fine demonstration of the Chinese wealth and influence in the region.

It was easy to meander around central Georgetown, discovering new delights around every corner. If my legs became a little weary, finding a welcoming little place for a coffee or a cold drink was a simple task.

I pushed the boat out for my evening meal by visiting the Jaipur Court, the beautifully appointed restaurant opposite the Blue Mansion. The place which had caught my eye the previous day.

It had undergone a tasteful restoration with many original features kept and enhanced. This included the large red floor tiles, intricately carved mahogany screens and silently turning, beautiful old fans suspended from the high ceilings. Multiple pot plants, bamboo and water features provided a relaxed and refreshing atmosphere. They had excellent carvings, statuary, paintings and other objets d'art displayed to best advantage throughout the dining rooms at ground and first floor levels and on the wide staircase. The style was predominantly British Colonial, with a nod towards Chinese, Indian, Malay and even Thai influences.

The Head Waiter ushered me to my spot as a single diner. He then quickly brought a drink and the menu. It was redolent of another age, and I enjoyed pretending to be someone used to living the high life rather than simply an ancient backpacker on a budget.

While I sipped my drink, a large party of Indian background entered the restaurant and took their place at an adjacent venerable and sizeable oval table. Elegantly attired ladies of a certain age, dressed in brightly coloured saris and well-spruced gentlemen, made up the party. They were all happily chatting; it was a birthday gathering, and I quickly discovered it was in honour of a small and slender matriarch celebrating her 95th birthday. Later, they sang a rousing version of *'Happy Birthday'* in English.

My meal was perfect, but in reality, I enjoyed my street food Tandoori Set as much as this more elaborate culinary offering.

Having toured central Georgetown extensively on foot, I hired a motorbike the next day to explore further afield. Taking out one of these machines was almost becoming second nature by now. Many places offered rentals. It was inexpensive, so it was a simple decision, giving so much flexibility and a change from being reliant on the timetables and idiosyncrasies of public transport.

I could manage greater distances than with a bicycle, which might have been another option. As it was so hot and sticky, I dismissed this thought.

I headed out of town along the northern coastline and past some pleasant beach resort areas. Penang seemed to be repackaging itself as more of a heritage and cultural destination rather than just another 'fly and flop' holiday location. The beaches and resorts were okay, but nothing remarkable, whereas Georgetown's unique historical and colonial attractions made it an exceptional port of call.

I cut inland, winding slowly up a series of hairpins. The air was cooler, the traffic lighter, and it was delightful being out on the open road, a sharp contrast to the raucous hubbub and searing heat of central Georgetown. I rode past a vast new reservoir, presumably catering to the region's domestic water requirements. Then, on my way down from the heights, taking care not to go too quickly as loose sand and gravel provided a regular skid hazard, I descended through verdant forested areas. I emerged on the coastal plain where villages of simple stilted wooden houses with rusting corrugated iron roofs were the norm.

I turned back inland past the airport and down to the impressive Penang Bridge, a 14.5km link to the mainland built in the mid-eighties. As I drew closer to the bridge, the traffic became heavier. This was not what I wanted, and as I negotiated the increasingly dense traffic on the outskirts of Georgetown, I was doubting the wisdom of choosing this route.

Rather than having the freedom of the open road, I was now suddenly in the middle of a classic Asian gridlock of hooting and honking vehicles. Scores of ancient jalopies were spewing out vast clouds of noxious fumes. The heat and pollution from the traffic added to the extremely high temperatures from the afternoon sunshine and made for some considerable discomfort. There were traffic lights every few hundred yards. We seemed to be kept waiting for minutes on end, while I carefully negotiated the many freight vehicles and hundreds of motorbikes.

I kept my cool (metaphorically speaking), ensuring that I was extra vigilant to avoid the many cavalier drivers (the majority, seemingly) for whom the rules of the road meant not a lot.

I finally got back to my guesthouse feeling pleased about the way I handled the hectic traffic situation with no mishaps, but, as is often the case, pride goes before a fall.

That evening, with the Six Nations Rugby Tournament kicking off back in Europe, I was keen to find somewhere to watch England's opening encounter away to Scotland. I quickly found a sports bar around the corner and watched England cruise to victory at Murrayfield with a subpar performance on a boggy pitch. Robinson grabbed a brace of tries with Cohen and Tindall adding others, the Scots just coming up with one successful penalty kick from a hatful of efforts. England were the underwhelming winners 29-3.

I had shared the rugby-watching experience with a few like-minded ex-pats, so, as is the required practice, we took a few drinks on board to celebrate the victory. This led to an inevitable late night.

The next day, in the late morning after a lie-in, trying to take the bike a few hundred yards back to the rental establishment, I had my comeuppance. I couldn't get the intransigent beast going normally, as the electric starter was virtually dead. I, therefore, had to resort to the kick-start. Being pretty much a novice with motorbikes, this ended up being a bit of a disaster. It was very reluctant to turn over, but finally, the engine spluttered into life. I gave a twist to the accelerator to clear it, but the machine was in gear and the bike shot down the road like a demented kangaroo. My feet were not up, so I could not hit the foot brake, and the handbrake was worse than useless. I was half on, half off and rapidly heading for busy Chulia Street with no control. The throttle was stuck open, and the engine roared like a strangulated hyena. I had no alternative but to abandon ship, throwing myself off and letting go of the handlebars. The street came up to hit me at all the usual contact points - knees, elbows and hands - the bike squealing away beside me.

"Shit!" was my immediate response.

The bike seemed okay. It was pretty ancient with a few dents anyway, so that was not an issue. Switching the screaming engine off, I checked myself out. Just a few scrapes - road rash, essentially. But I was seeping an impressive amount of claret, which should really be kept on the inside. Quickly, I put on a top to hide the damage as far as possible - I didn't want to arouse any suspicions when handing the bike back.

After restarting the infernal machine, I rode to the shop at a steady pace. The hire place was a moneychanger-cum-bookshop-cum-motorbike-rental establishment and was quite busy. I parked up nonchalantly, waited my turn in the queue, and smilingly handed over the keys and collected my deposit. All done and dusted with no hassle. Good!

The day was sweltering and sticky with a heavy cloud cover, and as I had had a late night and was feeling a little jaded and lacking in energy, I took things easy. I licked my wounds metaphorically and physically and spent a few hours in a succession of air-conditioned coffee shops and internet cafes reading, writing and attending to my emails.

By mid-afternoon, the temperature had become a little more bearable, and the sky had cleared. I had not yet visited Penang Hill, and as dusk was supposedly the best time to go up to this iconic landmark, I took a local bus up to the funicular station.

The infuriatingly slow bus weaved through the afternoon traffic, passing the Wat Chayamangkalaram Thai temple, home of a giant reclining golden Buddha, and the adjacent Dhammikarama Burmese temple. They built these unique places of worship on land gifted to the relevant communities by the British way back in 1795.

Eventually, we arrived at the cable railway station, having journeyed only about 10km in an hour. The funicular, built in the 1920s, gave access to Penang Hill, which in reality is a series of peaks topping out at some 833m. The British developed the place as a colonial hill station. A tranquil place giving respite from the often intense temperatures found at sea level.

I had toyed with walking up the hill. However, because of the rapidly approaching dusk, time was pressing, and anyway, a general feeling of inertia meant that a ride up the hill was an acceptable outcome. Before the railway access opened, coolies carried high-ranking officers sitting in sedan chairs up to the peak.

Reaching the summit via a halfway station change and a tunnel, I realised it was just about the right time. Dusk was falling and the lights of Georgetown were twinkling magically below. Standing for a while, I surveyed the scene before me, and tried to pick out the various landmarks.

Wandering around the hilltop past a couple of grand houses, a sanatorium, and a police station, I then followed signs to the twenties-era hotel. As there were sizeable numbers of people around, I decided to have a meal there and allow the crowds to disperse before taking the trip back down. The place looked a little tired and dated, but the views from the terrace where I had taken a seat were sublime.

Smart beach resort hotels I had ridden past a few days earlier sparkled below me. While looking to my right, I could see the whole of the electric wonderland of Georgetown laid out splendidly and mesmerisingly a couple of thousand feet below. Further to my right, where I had been negotiating the rush hour traffic recently on my recalcitrant motorbike, I could see the necklace of fairy lights illuminating the Penang Bridge over to the mainland. The streets and buildings of Butterworth twinkled beyond the bridge.

It was breathtaking, and I could enjoy the view in quiet serenity with only a dozen fellow diners joining me on the restaurant terrace. To make things even better, the food when it arrived was substantially better than I had envisaged it would be - a well-worthwhile detour, I concluded.

Back down at the bottom of the hill, I took a taxi back into town, not wishing to endure a slow bone-shaking trip by public bus. Then in central Georgetown, I found a trendy western bar showing Liverpool's away annihilation of Leeds. The broadcast of Ireland's thrashing of a poor Welsh side in the Six Nations tournament followed this to round off my day.

Unbelievably, the Welsh leaked 54 points, disintegrating in the face of a decent challenge from a slick Irish outfit who were next up for England. Where I would find to watch that game, I did not know.

Chapter 3

INDONESIAN HIGHS AND LOWS

Having given up on any ideas of working my passage, so to speak, to get down the Malaysian Peninsula, I took a ferry across to the massive island of Sumatra. I would look at what Indonesia offered. So, in between watching the sport on television and sipping my pint, I was browsing maps and guides to see what the possibilities were.

My stay in Georgetown had been most enjoyable, and it was definitely a place I wanted to revisit, but it was now time to move on. I boarded the ferry for Medan over the Malacca Straits the following day.

Strong sunshine had rapidly burned off the early morning mist. Laying out on the deck was the best option because of the comfortable temperature, owing to the sea breeze. This way, I could spend the four-and-a-half-hour passage pleasantly enough - dozing, sunbathing and reading.

On arrival, officials herded me, along with scores of other travellers, into a vast customs hall and made us wait, standing, in stifling heat. Soon numerous rivulets of sweat were beading down my body, my legs were cramping and I was becoming decidedly uncomfortable. The extensive delay amid hordes of less-than-fragrant fellow travellers was not the best of introductions to the country. The officious port administrators were trying to organise some free bus transportation into the city but when it failed to materialise, were just happy to keep us standing there waiting.

And waiting.

Eventually, they let us all go, but there was still no transportation to take us to town. I sneaked on to a coach provided by another ferry line, which was an excellent result. Unfortunately, the air conditioning was not working, and being just above the equator meant that the midday temperature was hot enough to roast a lizard.

The traffic was gridlocked, so we spent the next couple of hours frying on a crappy bus, edging extremely slowly into Medan. With time passing, my plan to get a bus onwards to Berastagi was fast becoming a non-runner.

Medan, I was not finding attractive at this stage, either. Two million people lived in the city. It was noisy, hot, smelly, polluted, drab, and dirty, so it had little to commend it. It was a shithole.

The bus dropped me somewhere in the middle of a desolate urban sprawl. I began searching for somewhere to stay, desperately in need of divesting myself of the rucksack, having a good long shower, changing into some fresh clothes and finding somewhere for a cold beer.

Trudging for a mile or so without a sniff of anything like a guesthouse or hotel, I decided I needed a different solution. The continuing fierce heat and my increasingly (so it seemed) heavy pack were making progress tortuous.

Luckily a becak, a motorbike sidecar combination used as a taxi in those parts drew alongside. The driver was helpful and reckoned he could help me out. He found me an unprepossessing place opposite Medan's major attraction, the Mesjid Raya Mosque.

I had to lower my already basic standards. The place was shoddy, and I had to ask for clean bedding to go on to the sagging mattress, the existing sheets having shown disconcerting signs of not being freshly laundered. But the shower was powerful, and the place would do for a night.

After showering and changing, which made me feel a lot better, I ventured out. There was nowhere for a beer; the place was dryer than the Sahara in a sandstorm. By now, I was getting hungry; I stopped off at a cheap local fast-food franchise with a point-and-pick menu and selected something that I washed down with a lukewarm anaemic coffee. The basic grub did the job without getting anywhere near tickling my taste buds, and I continued on my quest for a cold beer.

The air was cooler, and I was more comfortable walking by this time. I trudged several miles, finding nothing. I passed many scruffy local cafes, Dunkin' Donuts, KFCs and Mcdonalds', but there were no welcoming bars.

A local who spoke English and was keen to engage in conversation suggested somewhere called the Equatorial, a supposed pub within the Novotel Hotel. I gave it a go. I found it a joke. There was a bar but no beer. A seven-piece band dressed in maroon crushed velvet suits were crooning old fifties tunes (in English) to a bored audience of three or four locals.

I abandoned it all as a poor job, deciding on an early night with my book.

The call to prayer from the huge mosque opposite awoke me at some ridiculous pre-dawn hour. I should have realised this might happen when I first realised the location of my accommodation.

The muezzin seemed to go on for ages - taking great pride, it seemed, in being loud, monotonous and continuous. Sleep was almost impossible afterwards, and although I must have dozed a little, I decided I might as well get up. I would have to get a bit of kip when travelling.

I caught an opelet, a minibus that worked like the 'request' songthaews in Thailand, to the bus station where I immediately saw a bus almost ready to depart for Berastagi. Someone quickly hoisted my rucksack up on top, where several young lads were sitting, and

I jumped inside. The bus was a colourfully painted wooden-bodied affair with bench seats across virtually the total width of the vehicle. Crammed in tightly, I was pleased it was only a journey of only an hour and a half or so.

My head was just a few inches from the roof, so I could not see a lot as I was above the window line. Also, as I could not anticipate the frequent potholes, I had to learn to react to them quickly and carefully to fracturing my skull.

At Berastagi, at the end of a journey that was probably better than expected, I immediately found the Wisma Sabayak guesthouse. This place looked and indeed turned out to be a professionally run establishment with welcoming staff.

I went a little upmarket with my room choice as I favoured a Western-style loo over the alternatives. The room with a large, fully tiled en suite bathroom also boasted a balcony looking over to the town and beyond towards Mt Sibayak. The latter was one of the two impressive volcanoes in the area. Still marginally active, it had last erupted in 1881. The second, at 2400m, a slightly higher peak, Mt Sinabung, was just out of sight, although unfortunately, low clouds and mist obscured much of view, anyway.

I had intended to climb one of the two volcanoes in the area, but if the current weather persisted, it would not be possible. Or at least it would be pointless and potentially dangerous. For now, I contented myself with a walk around town. The main road, Jalan Veteran, ran right through the middle of the straggling settlement. A few dusty side tracks were running off the main drag, but that was the extent of the place.

The town was in the Karo Highlands and sat at the height of some 1300m. The elevation meant that it was substantially less hot and steamy than the cauldron that was Medan. This was presumably why wealthy people from the city owned a few substantial properties dotted around. They used the town and the surrounding area as a weekend 'hill station' retreat to escape the oppressive city heat and high pollution levels.

The area was tremendously fertile, evidenced by the vast and attractively colourful displays of fruits and vegetables on stalls in the central market.

"You try, Sir? Very nice!"

A friendly old lady stallholder who smiled to reveal a decidedly sparse array of teeth persuaded me to drink a local speciality drink, maquisa, or passion fruit juice. Being so dentally challenged was hardly a recommendation for her product, but what the hell? It was indeed delicious.

There were enormous pyramids of a whole range of citrus fruits, passion fruit, avocados, and a vast selection of vegetables. Chayote (a type of gourd) and many other items I did not recognise were also featured in the displays.

I found the local Batak architecture fascinating. In the villages, as we approached Berastagi, I noticed several prime examples of the building style. In town, there were more and grander examples of houses built with 'buffalo horn' roofs dipping in the middle. They also had steep, intricately carved and coloured triangular wooden gables sloping in towards the houses.

Whereas Medan was a devout Muslim area, here, religion was very much a mixed bag. There were a sizeable number of Christians (Catholics and Protestants), Muslims and local Karo minority tribes who primarily practised animism. Some of the Christian restaurants in town advertised pork dishes that would not be on offer in Medan.

Another toothless old lady approached me.

"Are you Christian or Muslim?"

I answered tentatively, "Christian."

"Catholic or Protestant," she continued.

"Protestant," I replied, which seemed to satisfy her on the religious front, though the direct questioning continued.

"You married?"

"Separated," I shot back.

"Children?"

"Yes."

"How old are you? Do you have a big dick?"

I felt it was time to be moving on.

I found a pleasant enough little place to eat, chose the pork dish of the day because I could, and enjoyed a range of beautiful, tasty vegetables and salad accompaniments. It was terrific to savour the freshness, and the meal made a delightful change from the more usual and occasionally bland rice stir-fries. The meal in this modest restaurant was bursting with flavour. I could also have a beer.

I wandered on, feeling replete. Groups of large white egrets, or perhaps storks, on the higher buildings and trees surveying the scene, intrigued me as I explored further. Finding a bar, I stopped for a second beer. I watched some Premiership football, but when that was over, and the owner turned the volume to the max and put on a violent all-action movie, I moved on.

Other bars seemed to go for the same form of entertainment, with a small audience of slack-jawed, blank-faced young locals staring at the screen.

So, I went to investigate my guesthouse's sister business, which was in the middle of Jalan Veteran, to check the noticeboard and see whether there were any tour options. Scaling one of the volcanoes did not seem workable as the low cloud and overcast conditions continued to prevail.

As I walked into the reception area, a couple of young Dutch women and their Canadian travel companion, a guy in his mid-twenties, were talking with a petite dark-haired lady who was smiling agreeably from behind the desk.

"That is a bit expensive. Can you do it cheaper?" the taller Dutch girl said to the guesthouse manager.

"You need more people. Then cheaper each person," the manager explained reasonably.

"Hi, I'm John; I may be interested in a trip. What's involved?" I pushed myself into the conversation, but it seemed okay.

The proposed trip I learned was a minibus excursion for the next day to see a Karo village, some of the surrounding countryside, and visit some hot water volcanic springs. This plan seemed acceptable, and within a couple of minutes, I agreed to join them on the trip. We settled the price at a reasonable compromise.

*

I had found the previous evening that my sparkling and spacious bathroom did not offer hot water, so I had made do with a brief lukewarm splash. Not being a fan of cold showers. The next morning, with a distinct chill in the air, I availed myself of a mandi. A mandi is where, for a small fee, the establishment would provide a large bowl of hot water, along with a jug and a glorified washing-up bowl to stand in. After soaping oneself, the pitcher is used to rinse off. In reality, quite a civilised and enjoyable experience.

All suitably scrubbed up, I met with my fellow travellers, and the four of us clambered into a new comfortable minibus and set off. It all seemed pretty laid back, and it appeared we would have a decent input into the itinerary and the timings.

The countryside was lush and highly fertile, with small allotment-sized patches of land producing maize, potatoes, citrus fruits, salad vegetables and coffee and tea for good measure.

Livestock such as cattle, water buffalo, pigs, goats and chickens were everywhere. The country might have been poor in Western financial terms, but the locals were indeed wealthy in terms of provenance. Most lived a subsistence lifestyle but could sell surpluses at market, which enabled them to purchase consumer goods such as clothing, furniture, televisions and satellite dishes - the latter being ubiquitous.

Our first planned stop was a Karo village with a traditional longhouse. However, the 'rumah adat', to give it its traditional name, was in a sad state of repair. There were many holes in the moss-covered thatch, and the visit was a bit of a damp squib.

We turned up trumps further on when we reached the village of Desa Lingga. The traditional settlement of some 2500 Karo people was in a time warp where the inhabitants continued living the way of life their antecedents had done for centuries.

Usually, Lingga was a popular backpacker attraction, but the four of us were the only visitors, as it was still early morning. The Deputy Head Man, an educated chap who had trained as an architect, met us and showed us around. He explained he had returned to his roots under the terms of some government-sponsored scheme to help preserve the traditional skills and lifestyle of the Karo. As a highly trained professional with technical skills, he was in charge of a programme of reconstruction and maintenance for the village.

"My father was a carpenter and handled most of the original building work here," he told us, opening out his arms to show off the magnificent longhouses. Unlike the single dilapidated house of the previous village, in Lingga, the rumah adats were in tip-top condition with gilded, painted, and carved triangular end walls glistening in the morning sunshine. The thatched roofs were in excellent order and topped with the ever-present buffalo horns. He was obviously, and rightly, proud of his heritage and his work.

The huge longhouses were home to up to eight families, all with four independent cooking hearths. Two families would share the cooking facilities. There were no internal walls. Sometimes they placed drapes up at night to give some privacy, but that was about the extent of it. Toilet facilities were basic and external.

At around seventeen, they sent the young lads of the village to sleep in a separate 'bachelor pad' to prevent possible sexual shenanigans. Teenage girls remaining in the longhouse would sleep by the outside walls so that they could hear the boys coming 'a courting'.

A young man would play his unique tune on a flute to identify himself to the girl he wanted to woo. After relating this tale, our guide gave a rendition of his own courting tune. He had whisked a flute from his pocket and serenaded us with a bright little melody.

We moved on from Lingga, taking a muddy, badly rutted and winding road uphill and down dale to reach the base of the impressive Gunung Sinabung. The mountain stuck up from the surrounding countryside like a giant pimple with its head in the clouds. We sidetracked to a beautiful tranquil lake with magnificent views of the volcano's lower slopes, but the persistent misty conditions obscured the higher reaches.

After a nasi goreng late lunch in the nearby town of Kabanjahe, we drove from the base of one volcano to the bottom of the other one, Sibayak. The idea was to visit the hot sulphur springs. By now, the heavy cloud had descended. Visibility was poor and taking this trip rather than trying to tackle an ascent of a volcano seemed more than pragmatic.

Our guide took us to an unattractive series of concrete tanks wreathed in foul-smelling sulphurous fumes. He then invited us to paddle or bathe in the waters, which were at different temperatures. He assured us this would be beneficial for our health. The four of us were less than convinced.

"You are joking. It stinks," was the general conclusion.

We headed back via a serendipitous meeting with a single alpha male baboon who was sitting by the roadside nonchalantly grooming himself.

Overall, the day was an enjoyable excursion and a relaxing way of experiencing the way of life in the Karo Highlands.

We shared a couple of beers on our return at a bar on the main road, but with everyone having dawn travel plans, early nights were in order. Not that there was much on offer in downtown Berastagi to encourage us to stay out.

*

It was time to move on to Lake Toba, a place I had been told about by fellow travellers on the banana pancake trail. It was a beautiful place with a tranquil vibe and would be a great place to relax for a few days.

First thing in the morning, I piled into a locals' opelet bound for Kabanjahe bus station, sharing the space with about fourteen competitive smokers. I was glad to be by the open door.

There were scores of dilapidated buses at the depot with conductors rushing about, shouting and herding people to their designated vehicles. I was looking to head for Siantar and then on to Parapat. Beyond Parapat, it would be a short ferry trip to the island of Samosir in the middle of Lake Toba.

After a bit of a shouting match, they directed me to the right bus. A young lad, the driver's assistant, slung my rucksack up on top and lashed it down and I piled in to grab the back seat. The bus was only three-quarters full at this stage, so I spread out and had the comfort of a decent bit of legroom.

The bus did not remain so spacious for long. We stopped frequently and picked more and more people up so that the vehicle became laughably overcrowded. A gangly local chap stood next to me, almost bent double, his head regularly bashing the roof as we hit one of the constant potholes. He hurled vehement abuse at the conductor, who, to stop the tirade, squeezed him in somewhere else.

It was due to be a three-hour trip, but who knew? It could be longer. My modus operandi was to enter a calm Buddha-like frame of mind, switch off from reality, and enter a pleasant world of reverie. On this journey, I ended up playing a slow game of twister with a total stranger.

I was the only Westerner on board. One lady, a nurse by the look of her uniform, with an ample bosom and a smiling face, seemed happy enough to end up next to me. Her elbow rested in my crotch, and my arm was in between her breasts, but she seemed quite content with the arrangement.

At Siantar, where there had been a recent deluge, the place was a mud bath. Huge puddles a foot or more deep covered the deeply rutted road. The driver had to negotiate the vehicle with care through the mini-lakes as we approached the bus station.

At the depot, it was absolute mayhem, with decrepit old coaches, minibuses and motorcycles all over the place. On finally descending from our vehicle, a noisy crowd of locals screaming advice about accommodation, tourist trips and onward transportation surrounded me. Standing a foot taller than most of them, I shouted to them to shut up, waved them away dismissively with my arm, and walked on purposefully. Slinging my rucksack over my shoulder as I marched off, I inadvertently swiped a few of the persistent touts out of the way.

I didn't quite know what I was going to do. My conclusion was that I needed to get away from the melee. And not be on a bus for a while.

Food would be a good option, as I had had no breakfast. I quickly found a kindly looking middle-aged woman at a food stall on the perimeter of the vast muddy expanse. She seemed honoured to serve a Westerner at her humble little café and fussed about seating me at the best table. The lovely lady quickly brought me a drink before rustling up a delicious spicy stir-fry featuring some exotic vegetables.

After taking my time over the food and relaxing with my book for a while, I decided Siantar did not warrant any further exploration, and I would continue my journey. After a bit of investigation, I found a minibus was due to leave shortly for Parapat. I paid and handed in my ticket. The driver took my bag and gestured for me to sit next to two young women in the middle seat.

The girls seemed pleasant and keen to chat, and they spoke good English. They introduced themselves to me as sisters, Muni and Rinis, 22 and 20, who had been visiting the morning market and were now going home to Samosir. We chatted about where I had travelled and where I was going, and I asked them about their way of life. The conversation flowed, and the journey passed most agreeably. It was just as well, as my head was stuck in the roof, and I could see none of the passing scenery.

As we approached Parapat, we dropped steeply and spectacularly; we were descending the edge of a caldera, the blown-off top of an erstwhile volcano.

The super-volcanic event which formed the caldera took place some 75,000 years ago. It was so devastating that some experts have suggested that the catastrophe reduced the world's population to just a few thousand. It was a major, major event.

Lake Toba now filled the hole left by the ancient seismic cataclysm, a substantial lake of over 100km in length and with parts reaching over 500m deep.

Once in Parapat, as we needed to take a ferry across Lake Toba to the island of Samosir - almost as large as Singapore - the girls showed me the ropes.

The timing was good as the car ferry was filling up and due to leave in about ten minutes. Muni explained we were to cross as foot passengers, a journey of about an hour, and then just take a local bus along the lakeside for a few miles. The sisters suggested I stay at the laid-back and traveller-friendly lakeside village of Tuk-Tuk - they would show me where to get off the bus. I wrote details of a guesthouse they could recommend in my notebook.

A large and colourfully painted antiquated ferry, with a charming necklace of decorated tyres draped along its sides, throbbed and spluttered into action, and we were underway. Shimmering in the sunlight, the lake was a deeply vibrant ocean blue. Having put in a recent appearance, the sun was most welcome, although clouds still obscured all but the lowest hills. It was a pleasant way to travel, the gentle breeze crossing our bows and the soporific hum of the engines as we breached the white tops making me drowsy after my long day of travelling. There was even room to move about and a little snack bar where I bought myself and the sisters a coffee. The coffee did the job of stopping me from dozing.

Once docked, we quickly found another overcrowded minibus for the ride along the lakeside road. Muni and Rinis gave me their address, which was just along the lake a little way, and insisted I drop in to see them. I promised I would. They got the minibus driver to stop at a junction, and I was suddenly alone at the roadside. Just a ten-minute walk away from Tuk-Tuk, I was told.

Some ten minutes, I thought as I shifted my rucksack to a more comfortable position. I had been walking getting on for half an hour when a motorbike taxi came along. I gratefully accepted the lift, particularly when I found the place I was heading for was on the far side of the long straggling village we were just entering.

Mas Guesthouse was lovely, a neat little house with well-kept lakeside gardens and clean and spacious rooms, but it was a little remote. Tuk-Tuk had looked from the back of the motorbike to be an interesting backpacker-orientated place with several bars and restaurants. There were also craft shops, cycle and motorbike hire establishments and tour operators. I probably needed to be closer to the action.

After settling in, I borrowed a bike from the young son of the house and rode a couple of miles back into the centre of town. Riding past a string of lakeside guesthouses, all with beautiful gardens filled with lush, colourful blooms stretching down to the water, I was enthralled by the place. It was idyllic. So far removed from Medan, it was like a completely different country.

I was very much taken with Tuk-Tuk and decided to move closer to town for the next few days. I checked out a couple of bars, had a good wander about, and concluded that the place was coming up trumps.

It was pulsating, lively and colourful, with a lot going on. More than a few travellers were about, so I felt it would be great to meet up with people and swap travel stories.

However, the friendly guesthouse owner back at Mas had insisted on preparing an evening meal for me, so I had gone along with that. I pedalled back and had an enjoyable dinner with the family before gently letting them know I would move out the next day.

In the morning, all the clouds had disappeared, and the clear blue sky revealed a wonderful and spectacular secret. Beyond the narrow plain alongside the lake and the small gently rising hills, the mountains, previously unseen, soared up steeply and majestically to around three hundred metres. I could see the steep grey escarpment slashed by a cascading silvery waterfall, tumbling down hundreds of feet. Looking in the other direction down the garden, a fisherman paddled noiselessly in his basic dugout boat on the lake, the waters looking cool, mirror-like and inviting. The entire scene was mesmeric.

Feeling refreshed from a good night's sleep and energised by the warm sunshine and clear skies, I decided to walk into Tuk-Tuk after breakfast.

I strolled through to the other side of the snaking village in search of accommodation and eventually found a beautiful guesthouse. The traditional lakeside house, complete with three or four impressive pet iguanas in the garden, would be ideal.

"They live for a long while. Twenty years or longer. They are very calm normally, but they can bite!" The owner told me.

Over a coffee, I chatted with Tag, the amiable landlord of the house and keeper of the iguanas. He told me that when I wanted to leave, he could phone the ferry company, and they would pick me up from the stone dock at the bottom of his garden. Very convenient.

I wanted to explore and get a bit of exercise, so I walked back into the centre of the settlement and quickly hired a decent mountain bike for the day. I intended to pop in to see the girls from the ferry and then discover further afield. A day in the saddle would make a pleasant change.

I easily found the sisters' home a few miles along the road, a modestly sized wooden house on short stilts right on the lakeside. They welcomed me in like a long-lost friend.

"Hi. Lovely to see you, John. This is Raja, our brother; sit down here. Would you like a cup of coffee? We have told Raja all about you."

The house had polished hardwood floors and wood-panelled walls, with minimal furniture. They did, however, have a range of electronic equipment, the latest stereo gear, and a large-screen television. They had pictures on the wall, a little incongruously, of Jesus Christ alongside Bob Marley and Slash from Guns "n" Roses.

That would make a good band, I thought.

Raja was friendly and keen to help me explore his home area, of which he seemed proud.

"I could take you out up to the Tele Observation Point, at the top of the mountains tomorrow if you would like," offered Raja.

"Fantastic views."

"You can easily get a motorbike in Tuk-Tuk."

"Yes, that sounds good," I replied.

And we fixed it. On the following day, I would show up at 10.

After finishing my coffee, and having a general chitchat about life in the area, I was on my way.

I followed the gently undulating lakeside road past grazing water buffalo and orchards, growing a prolific range of tropical and citrus fruits. The fields of various crops were being tended by family groups. I came across dusty little villages with pigs, chickens, and toddlers scurrying around while languorous cats observed the scene with their normal air of superiority. Gardens were blooming with abundant, luxuriant and colourful plants - rich pinks, purples, yellows, and scarlets. On the lake and the shoreline, fisherfolk were busying themselves with their various tasks.

I cycled past loads of family vaults and ornate graveside memorials in the corners of fields. It seemed to be the pattern here rather than deceased relatives being laid to rest in large communal cemeteries.

At one point, I saw a large tree filled with twenty-odd cranes, just sitting there grooming their feathers. Further along, I rode through a thick spider's web, the most significant piece of arachnid construction I had ever seen - it spread right across the road. I stopped to investigate and could see several spiders, two or three inches across, lying in wait for some tasty prey. Some sort of cooperative spider community effort must have been responsible for the construction of the web.

I later came across several good examples of traditional Batak houses with intricately painted gables and roofs adorned with buffalo horns. Later, I passed a 'Chief's House', in tip-top order, which was now operating as a small museum.

I stopped off for a late and ubiquitous nasi goreng lunch at an attractive little restaurant on the lakeside, before resting in the sun for a while and then heading back to base.

In Tuk-Tuk for the evening, I checked out a few bars and chatted with some travellers. Later, I enjoyed a decent meal and found a live music backpacker-orientated venue to round off a full and enjoyable day.

After breakfast on the terrace with the iguanas, I readily picked up a motorbike in Tuk Tuk and headed off to meet Raja.

"Looks good, John," he said enthusiastically when I met him - I could see the new gleaming red machine I had parked outside of the house impressed him. The vehicle was something I knew he aspired to own but could not currently afford.

He seemed pleased as he leapt into the saddle and fired up the engine, gesturing for me to get on the pillion seat, and off we went.

Much to my relief, I quickly established he was a competent rider and not as gung ho as some other locals. I could relax on the back and take in the views.

We travelled along the lakeside. The terrain was initially reasonably flat as we rode below the towering mountains with the glistening lake on our right. Suddenly Raja made an abrupt left turn, and we headed steeply upwards around a constant succession of hairpin bends. The road climbed inexorably for several miles, with sheer drops on one side and vertical rock walls on the other.

I was pleased Raja took things reasonably cautiously. One heart-in-the-mouth moment came, though, when we went around a blind bend when a massive glistening black water buffalo, casually chewing the cud in the middle of the road, blocked our passage. We swerved around the unusual obstacle as he glared at us nonchalantly and continued up to the top.

The Tele Observation Point offered stunning and extensive views of the lake, the surrounding mountains and the villages below. We could see Lake Toba, the largest volcanic lake in the world, in all its glory. We could also see much of the island of Samosir, the largest island within an island in the world. As Samosir itself boasted a couple of sizeable lakes, we were looking at lakes on a large island in a vast lake on the island of Sumatra.

We had a spot of lunch at the little café/restaurant at the top and a stroll around, enjoying the awe-inspiring views, before steadily taking the twisting and precipitous route back.

*

Over the last couple of days, many of the restaurants in Tuk-Tuk advertising mushroom omelettes, as their house speciality had intrigued me. On further enquiring of some travellers, it was apparent that these mushrooms were a magical specialism - and they could sell the psychedelic fungi legally.

I thought I might give it a bit of a whirl and found a nice-looking restaurant.

After a while, having enjoyed my mushroom omelette, chips and salad, I began tripping gently, some wonderfully vibrant technicolour images dancing before my eyes.

By this time, I was talking to a couple of Aussie travellers, Rod and Josie. They seemed to be happy enough chatting with an ancient tripping hippy. We had a pleasant and convivial evening as far as I could remember. The alcohol combined well with the mushrooms for a most intoxicating and psychedelic experience. My new friends were much amused with my explanations of what I was encountering. I was giving a running commentary describing the intense other-worldly shapes and vibrant, kaleidoscopic colours dancing before my eyes.

My most enjoyable stay on Lake Toba was ending, and the following day, I woke early to get ready for my appointment with the ferry. The guesthouse owner, Tag, assured me he had everything organised and I should just sit on his little stone quay and wait. So after a last goodbye to him and the iguanas, I did just that.

It was a beautifully peaceful morning with barely a breeze rippling the clear blue waters lapping gently at the stone wall a few feet below where I sat. The mountains on the far side of the lake, several miles away, looked close enough to touch.

Looking back towards the handsome house, home for the last three or four days, I contemplated the rich, colourful splendour of Tag's lovingly tended garden. My eyes, vision possibly enhanced and heightened by the mushrooms, feasted on the deep lilacs, vibrant golds, oranges and scarlets.

I watched as, a couple of houses along, a young mother was wrestling a toddler in the lake shallows, forcibly washing the complaining, howling and unamused infant.

A toot from the ferry coming into the dock shook me from my reverie.

Chapter 4

TRAVELLING TO SINGAPORE

I was resigned to a long day of potentially uncomfortable travelling. Bukittinggi, my next port of call on my way down to Singapore, was, according to different sources, eleven to eighteen hours away along rough and mountainous roads. I had also learned that the tourist bus was not running, so I would have to travel by the local bus service.

When I reached the bus station in Parapat, I found I had a few hours to wait. There was some confusion about what buses were running, but officials assured me nothing would arrive until noon.

The depot was an expanse of rough open tarmac about a hundred metres square with just a few little bars and cafés on the periphery. It all looked more than a little run down, so I walked back down to the much more attractive waterfront area to explore.

After a mid-morning brunch and a further stroll, I meandered back to the bus area, enjoying the magnificent lake and mountain views. Noon came and went, with no sign of any vehicle. At around 1.30 pm, whilst having a cold drink and reading my book at a pleasant little bar, a likely-looking contender finally turned up.

I abandoned my drink and legged it over to where the bus had drawn to a halt about a hundred yards away. As a young lad was at that moment cleaning my shoes, this was a painful experience, running barefoot over the rutted, stony and spectacularly hot surface. Sod's law meant I quickly established this was not my bus. I had to return to the bar doing the Mexican hat dance on the way back, much to the amusement of some locals sitting outside.

About forty minutes later, my bus turned up. It was almost full of locals and supplemented with about half a dozen backpackers.

For the first five hours, the ancient charabanc wound up and down the mountains, swinging around extremely tight bends with virtually no straight sections. Deeply rutted and potholed, the poor condition of the road made progress tediously slow. The net result was a most uncomfortable gut-wrenching, nausea-inducing, rolling, bumpy ride more akin to being on a small yacht in a force eight rather than on a coach journey. One poor lad of about five a couple of seats in front of me managed to projectile vomit all over his dad, which did not improve the ambience. It wasn't very pleasant for his dad, either.

Reading was impossible, so I tried to relax into a zen-like state and look out at the magnificent equatorial rain forests stretching up the mountainsides and the deep green terraced paddy fields in the valleys. When darkness came, sleep was not possible with the coach's extreme swinging motion, so it was just a matter of trying to lose myself in thought.

We had some stops where people got on and off. We also hung around for twenty minutes at one point when the driver's young assistant disappeared under the vehicle with a heavy-duty spanner to effect some running repairs. Progress was slow.

Passenger numbers were by now reduced to the level where I could commandeer the back seat and spread out as the hours rolled by. I got a couple of hours of uncomfortable sleep.

I was awake at around 4 am when we pulled into Bukatinggi. Not that I would have recognised the place, but the second driver assured me this was where I needed to get off. It was the middle of nowhere.

There were scores of taxis flocking around the bus like vultures, with drivers demanding (relatively) enormous sums for undisclosed journeys to God knew where. I gave them a miss. Grabbing my rucksack, I headed off down the road.

I saw a sign for a hotel up a narrow lane and followed it. I quickly came across a vast four or five-star upmarket resort hotel with an open-plan layout of elegant guest bungalows set amongst manicured lawns. There was no one in sight, no night porter or any security personnel. I toyed with the idea of looking around to find a sun lounger on the poolside to bed down for what remained of the night. I discounted this idea quickly, as I thought this might lead to arrest or even summary execution. So I settled for getting my sleeping bag out and bedding down on a pleasant, flat grassy area opposite the hotel.

Nicely into a deep sleep for what seemed like five minutes, the inevitable morning call to prayer woke me abruptly. Loud, piercing and discordant and coming from at least half a dozen different sources, this signalled the end of my sleep. Dozing a little as this first instalment relented, I was soon re-awoken when the 6.30 call started. Packing up my sleeping bag, I gave it all up as a poor job.

At that moment, I heard a friendly voice from across the road. A security chap from the hotel was beckoning. He was very interested in knowing where I was from and where I was going. Having gained his confidence, I cheekily asked if I could use a loo. He was happy with this and walked me over to the poolside changing block. He showed me the shower area. It was all so well appointed and I enjoyed an excellent long, hot and reviving shower.

Feeling revitalised despite only a fitful couple of hours of sleep, after warmly thanking my benefactor, I walked off down the track to the main road. Here I could hail an opelet to the bus station. I was heading directly on to Pekanbaru and then somehow to Singapore.

I was now at around 930m above sea level (and incidentally in the Southern Hemisphere, after crossing the equator at some stage in the night), so the air was clear and fresh.

Before my bus slot, I had a small window of opportunity to explore the market district and the area around the giant clock tower, Jam Gadang. This is Bukatinggi's modest claim to fame. Ornate carriages pulled by patient fly-blown horses waited there for tourists. They call the rigs 'bendis'.

The bus journey was another lengthy, twisting, mountainous trek of some five or six hours, but the driver seemed to get a move on when he could. The topography flattened out in the last hour of the trip, and we journeyed through a wide valley of palm groves and rubber plantations. On the town's outskirts, there were several extensive timber yards.

Pekanbaru was less than enchanting. It was a dump. Almost literally, as refuse piled up high all over the place. Walking around was hazardous as sewer covers were missing, leaving gaping holes down into stinking cesspits. In some areas, workers had cleared rubbish from these voids and left it to dry in the sun. Delightful.

Eventually, I secured somewhere to stay the night, but the town reminded me of Medan. Not a great recommendation. Guesthouses, or 'losmen', were shabby, toilets and showers were barely adequate, and bedding did not look fresh. I selected the best I could find on offer. However, I slept in my sleeping bag and was quite circumspect about using the facilities.

It was also very much like Medan with finding somewhere for a meal or, heaven forbid, a beer. However, the losmen proprietor could secure me a speedboat ticket over to Batam, which saved me the hassle of trying to work it all out in the morning. Batam is a small Indonesian island close to Singapore accessed by small, fast boats which depart from Pekanbaru's river port.

After a pretty forgettable evening, I headed off in the morning in a crappy old minibus to some sort of port 'office' (a run-down shack) for some ticket administration. Then a local bus went around the houses interminably before disgorging us at the river port. The departure area was a collection of dusty falling-down wooden huts surrounded by piles of refuse and a few purveyors of uninspiring street food. Their offerings seemed to be popular with the flies, though.

Travelling to Singapore

Eventually, we were underway, racing across the white-capped waves on our bumpy and noisy way to Batam. There were half a dozen of us in a tiny speedboat, the pilot of which was looking to break the world water speed record. And doing so while negotiating a route around vast tonnages of shipping in one of the world's busiest commercial sea lanes. He was not without skill and experience, though, and we made it with nothing untoward happening.

A quick transfer in Batam and I was on my way to Singapore on a more conventional ferry. We waited patiently outside the harbour some forty-odd minutes after leaving Indonesia whilst the impressive luxury liner '*White Star Virgo*' docked. I took in the remarkable skyline of one of the world's most iconic and vibrant port cities from the ferry's open deck. Tourists on the cable car going to Sentosa Island waved down at us.

It was not my first visit to Singapore. I had touched down in the city after visiting India and before going to Australia way back in the previous June. I then spent a couple of days after leaving Oz and starting my SE Asian foray some months later.

Before that, I had been on a rugby tour with my club Bracknell RFC back in '87. I had done a little exploring on these visits but felt that I had not done the place justice. I aimed to put that right on this trip, although my time would again be short.

When I had a stopover coming in from India, lengthened to about 16 hours from the planned 4 hours by some sort of hiccup with flights, I enjoyed the luxury of a 4-star hotel for the day plus generous meal vouchers. This time I would not be enjoying such a luxury.

With my newly gained city map, I set out for Chinatown to find some cheap lodgings. Singapore is very expensive, so I concluded that this would be the best place to find something a little more affordable. Finding a decent little guesthouse (which was much more expensive than what I had become used to in Indonesia), I dropped my bag off after completing the formalities. It was acceptable in the circumstances. Unencumbered, I headed out for a little investigative stroll.

My lodgings were close to Clarke Quay and Boat Quay and I checked them out, but found the area somewhat touristy, as I had expected. This area was the old commercial hub of Singapore, on the banks of the eponymous river. The beautiful old refurbished warehouses were now dwarfed by sparkling, new soaring glass and steel skyscrapers.

I found a little coffee shop around the corner, away from the tourist crowds, and stopped for a while, reflecting on Singapore's journey.

Sir Stamford Raffles founded modern Singapore - The Lion City in 1819. He intended to establish it as a British Empire trading post. This was accomplished by forging a close alliance with the local ruler, Sultan Hussein, the latter being awarded a generous stipend for his helpful attitude.

Singapore's darkest hour came in 1942 when the Japanese occupied the country, after taking Malaya, and after what was, according to Churchill:

"Britain's largest capitulation."

The date of the Allies' defeat by the Japanese at the Battle of Singapore was 15th February 1942. The next day, when I was due to leave Singapore for Hong Kong, would be 15th February 2002, exactly sixty years from that historic date.

After the defeat, the Japanese captured many thousands of Allied prisoners and put them into POW camps where they suffered indescribable indignities and deprivations, brutal tortures, starvation and summary executions.

The treatment of so many of the civilians was even more egregious. The Sook Ching massacre was a purge of ethnic Chinese civilians, and others thought to be anti-Japanese. Announcing themselves as liberators, freeing fellow Asians from the yoke of European colonial oppression, the Japanese were, in reality, abominably malevolent invaders. When they realised that the local population did not perceive them as liberators, they behaved with the utmost savagery and barbarism. Officials have calculated the number massacred to be between 10,000 up to perhaps 100,000. There are also horrific stories of the rape and murder of scores of Australian nurses and the wiping out of hospital staff and patients at the Alexandra Hospital. There was also the barbarous execution, or more accurately slaughter, of many Sikhs by Japanese soldiers casually taking potshots at them as target practice. The cruelty of the Japanese military during the war was beyond most human understanding.

After the Japanese surrender in 1945, they returned Singapore to British rule and the colonial outpost thrived as a major shipping and financial hub. The nation finally gained self-governance in 1959.

Today, Singapore, boasting the second-highest population density in the world after Macau, places favourably in many critical social and financial indicators. The city-state ranks highly in health, education, life expectancy, wealth (one in six families has dollar millionaire status), personal happiness, homeownership and security. They are incorrupt and meritocratic and their political machinery runs on Westminster principles.

There is rich cultural and ethnic diversity. They enshrine multiculturalism in the country's constitution. Most people speak two or even three languages; English is in the vanguard with Malay, Chinese, and Tamil widely spoken. However, and for me, there is an 'however', the authorities are prescriptive in terms of personal liberties. There is little press independence or freedom of speech and limited political and civil rights. The authorities are not too keen on drugs either. Being caught in possession of even small amounts of illegal recreational substances can lead to severe flogging and long-term incarceration in the notorious Changi jail.

A tee shirt worn by one brave young man I saw had bold lettering which stated, *'Singapore is a Fine City'*. Underneath in much smaller text was a list of the petty things for which the authorities would be more than happy to levy a fine. That just about summed Singapore up for me. Too squeaky clean, too paternalistic, too prescriptive, too controlling, a mecca to conspicuous consumption and the over-enthusiastic worship of the mighty dollar.

I finished my second cup of coffee and headed off. I walked over Elgin Bridge on South Bridge Road and looked across to the row of bars, pubs and restaurants attractively created from old warehouses of differing heights, widths and roof styles. The restaurants had canopied riverside seating, and all looked rather splendid as more people gathered in the early evening. To my left were a dozen impressive glittering towers heading skywards. I was sure they were not there in '87.

There were decorations and signage relating to the coming festivities celebrating the Chinese New Year of the Horse, with workers erecting more colourful Chinese lanterns, signs, balloons, and other paraphernalia. I saw several slogans exhorting *'real wealth is daring to make the most of yourself'* and other such notions.

Behind me, as I contemplated the river, was the handsome classical parliament building built in speckled grey polished marble. Further down was the Raffles landing site, where the great man first set foot on Singapore Island.

I suddenly realised it was Valentine's Day, not that it held any significance for me. I noticed quite a few smartly dressed, lovey-dovey couples walking along arm in arm, the young ladies all clutching identical little bouquets. Both the men and the women seemed to wear fixed smiles and be enjoying themselves by numbers. There was no form of spontaneity or individuality. They regularly took photos on their new-fangled, clever little phones, with which they seemed to be constantly referring. I looked immediately across to my left and saw a mixed group of half a dozen young locals at an outside table. All of them were transfixed by their mobile phone screens and taking constant photographs of their friends and themselves. It all seemed pretty incredible - these things would probably catch on back home soon.

Most of the couples were strolling to nearby restaurants, which reminded me I was ready for my evening meal. I headed back to Chinatown, where I intended to feast on an authentic and hopefully not expensive meal that would not break the bank.

I found just the right place close to my lodgings, and I enjoyed an excellent, relaxed dinner and a couple of beers. Wearied by the day's travelling and expecting a full last day in Singapore to come, I settled for an early night.

The next morning, if not exactly up with the lark, I was out and about early, appreciating the slightly cooler and fresher morning air. I strolled around somewhat aimlessly; stopping off at an attractive café for a breakfast coffee. I had a loose plan in mind to check out the famous Singapore Cricket Club, where I had played rugby in 1987.

After more meanderings and further admiring the mix of restored nineteenth-century buildings and exciting new skyscrapers, I approached the mightily impressive Padang. This large sports field became the centrepiece for colonial development in the days of Raffles. Opposite me, I could see the National Gallery and other fine colonial buildings, book ended by the Singapore Cricket Club and the Singapore Recreation Club.

I headed for the Singapore Cricket Club in the late morning sunshine and strode purposefully to the ornate marble entrance, where I spoke to a pleasant-natured uniformed doorman.

"Good morning", I offered, not quite knowing how I was going to proceed.

"I came here in 1987 with my rugby club to play against the cricket club rugby team."

(Whilst nominally a cricket club, the renowned institution was home to rugby, hockey, squash, soccer and tennis sections).

"I would love to have a look around for old time's sake. Would that be possible at all?"

He appraised me, and concluding that I appeared a solid and upright Englishman, replied smilingly,

"I am sure that would be alright. We are quiet at the moment. I will confirm."

Our club, which played at a relatively modest level back home, had been treated like royalty on our SE Asian tour. The visit to the splendid Singapore CC, playing on a perfect pitch surrounded by beautiful colonial buildings and enjoying an after-match reception more akin to a state banquet than the typical 'pie and beans,' had been a highlight of the trip.

The chap came back:

"Yes, that will be fine; I will take you in."

He showed me through the impressive entrance and introduced me to a manager who shook my hand warmly.

"A pleasure to have you here, sir," he said. "Please follow me."

I followed him up the wide curving staircase, past an array of action sporting shots and formal team photographs, up to the main reception room, known as the Padang Restaurant. Large windows afforded panoramic views of the lush green expanses beyond.

Many servers prepared tables for lunch, clinking cutlery and polishing and setting down cut glassware onto the spotless starched white tablecloths under the chandeliers. It took me straight back to my playing days - '87 being my swan song tour as a first-teamer. I had very fond memories of the players and officials from those times, many of whom I still regard as good friends. After the match, which we won, we enjoyed a formal dinner in these same surroundings, and I knew everyone appreciated being treated like we were the England squad.

It pleased me I had the cheek to ask for a tour of the facilities, and I found it an almost moving experience. Probably remembering myself and my teammates fit as fiddles and in the prime of life. Such a long time ago. I made sure I did not overstay my welcome and declined the offer of a drink before thanking my hosts profusely and moving on.

My next port of call was a little different. I was aiming for the world-famous Raffles Hotel. Once there looked for the renowned Long Bar where they had invented the Singapore Sling, and the habit of discarding peanut shells on the bar floor was more than encouraged. It disorientated me initially; I was heading for the ground floor room where I remember the bar being located, only to find a large reception area.

On enquiring, I was told that they had moved the Long Bar to the first floor. Rebuilt in the same style and still with mountains of peanut shells on the floor and people enjoying an early Singapore Sling, I found it but did not stay. I felt cheated. They had wiped the Long Bar I remembered from history.

The many luxury goods boutiques and Raffles' memorabilia outlets added to my conclusion that the hotel had sold its soul to Mammon, and I walked away disappointed.

Later, I walked around the Little India district and made a mental note that I would dine Indian style later, having enjoyed Chinese cuisine the previous evening. There were plenty of suitable restaurants by the look of things.

From teenagers to grandfathers, groups of men were hanging around on street corners chatting, smoking, and joking in the balmy afternoon sunshine. The area was a little shabby and poorer than the norm for Singapore, but it seemed a little more authentic.

Then I came across the fascinating Sri Mariamman temple, the city's oldest Hindu place of worship. The highly elaborate and colourful building, which was adorned with statues of multiple deities, looked spectacular, gleaming in the sunshine. Naraine Pillai, a government clerk from Penang who arrived in Singapore with Raffles in the late nineteenth century, was the man responsible for building the structure. The entrepreneurial Pillai later became very wealthy through his construction businesses as the city-state rapidly developed, and he was readily acknowledged as the leader of the region's Hindus.

Late afternoon, after repairing to my hostelry for a shower and change of clothes, I set out for my final evening in Singapore. I started by visiting the Equinox Tower, taking the express lift to the 71st floor for an over-the-top cocktail and a spectacular view across the fabulous cityscape at dusk.

It all looked quite magnificent, gazing out over the world's largest port and the busy waterways with the massive ships looking like toy boats from that height. I did not stay long because of slight vertigo and an aversion to prices as high as the tower itself.

Next, I checked out Chijmes, a former and stunningly beautiful Catholic convent building that had undertaken a fantastic conversion to provide a range of food, beverage and retail offerings. There was also considerable outdoor space with elaborately paved plazas, extensive planting and green areas. Chijmes seemed popular that evening with people enjoying a stroll, a drink or a meal.

After a relaxed beer and a spot of people-watching, I decided it was time for my Asian feast and headed off to Little India.

At a bustling place with lots of smiles, laughter, and mainly Indian families dining, I enjoyed an authentic meal washed down with a beer. Despite the relative poverty and apparent deprivation, life in Little India seemed fun.

Pleasantly full, I settled up the modest bill and headed back to the more touristy parts of town to see if I could discover a live music venue. When I visited Singapore on the rugby tour, I remembered I unearthed some excellent venues with highly talented local bands reproducing Western rock offerings. It was here I first came across radio mikes, enabling the lead singer to venture out into the auditorium unencumbered with trailing cables, still singing away. I couldn't fathom it out initially, concluding some oriental trickery or even miming. This latest technology was yet to reach our shores, lead singers having to put up with yards of intransigent cabling.

On this trip, I settled on the Voodoo Shack on Clarke's Quay. I was more than happy to have found a band fronted by an American rocker vocalist. He was ably supported by a superb Singaporean virtuoso lead guitarist, as well as locals on drums and bass. The band played through to midnight when I drained my last pint, said goodbye to my new acquaintances and wended my way back home to Chinatown.

I left in the morning for Changi Airport, taking a super clean, air-conditioned bus which cruised along smoothly, maintaining precisely the permitted 90kph, down the clear broad carriageway. Prolific amounts of colourful blooms and dark green foliage decorated the verges, central reservation area, and bridges. Everything was in pristine, tip-top Singaporean condition, reminding me somewhat of the approach drive to an American 5-star golf resort.

When I reached the airport, I noticed the signs on the automatic entrance doors had a long prescriptive list of what visitors could not do. It surprised me to see *'no studying'* was on the list. Presumably, they wanted to deter scruffy young students from sitting around all day on their laptops in what would be a very plush studying environment with all mod cons ready to hand.

I had a slight concern about how officialdom would view my severely distressed flight documents. They had never fully recovered from their lengthy immersion in the Ping River in Northern Thailand some months previously. As it had already passed muster, frequently, I was a little more sanguine about the battered passport. The document had caused comments by some jobsworths but had not prevented me from leaving or entering different countries.

My strategy was to arrive in good time, check in early and try to sweet talk a hopefully unpressured airline agent to let me have a boarding card without fuss. This plan worked to a degree as an attractive and smiling young lady employee wished me a good day and took the sorry-looking pile of papier mâché from me. She sympathised when I briefly explained what had happened. She then swiftly handed me a boarding card with no qualms after extracting the document relevant to the flight to Hong Kong from Singapore. This was not in too bad a condition.

However, she kept the rest of the documentation, including vouchers for other flight legs and my eventual homebound flight from Bangkok. She then asked me to wait, taking the remaining bundle off to the administration offices on the floor above.

After about ten minutes, it surprised me when a young man in an airline uniform startled me from my daydreaming.

"Sir," he said sharply.

"Oh. Good morning," I replied.

"Good afternoon," was his humourless response.

I checked my watch; it was two minutes past twelve.

He harangued and lectured me in a highly officious manner and told me in no uncertain terms that travel documents needed to be treated with the utmost care. I had singularly failed in that regard. Half expecting to be hauled up to see the headteacher and given six of the best, I almost looked around for a magazine to stuff down the back of my trousers to soften the expected blows.

He continued that if I needed to replace the damaged documents, I would have to go back into the city office and plead my case. He emphasised that officials there would not view this heinous crime lightly. I was at Changi Airport, but it would appear that they would soon send me next door to the notorious Changi Prison.

I took all this crap from the skinny little toerag, knowing that I had my boarding card safely in my pocket. However, the airline official still had my onward travel vouchers. I needed to be careful and not antagonise the little prick.

He then dramatically handed me back the offending documents, swivelled around, clicked his heels and, with an immaculately executed Nazi salute and a smart Heil Hitler, he was on his way.

I would deal with the matter later; I certainly had no intention of going back to the centre of Singapore.

Chapter 5
HONG KONG

We reached Hong Kong late afternoon, landing at Chek Lap Kok Airport, built at colossal expense and only completed four years earlier in 1998. They built the new construction on reclaimed land and significant chunks of the seabed. This project added a substantial 1% to Hong Kong's landmass. Lantau Island, the site of the new facility, is located to the north of the city.

The former Hong Kong Kai Tak airport, based in the densely populated Kowloon area with a single runway extending out to Kowloon Bay, was no longer fit for purpose. The terminus had huge issues with capacity, lengthy flight delays, and multiple other logistical problems. It also produced significant air and noise pollution levels, which directly affected the vast numbers of people living and working nearby.

We were, therefore, an hour's journey from the centre of the city. I had to wait a while to get a good view of this exciting, pulsating, and exotic city, which had been on my 'must-see' list for quite a time.

Travelling smoothly into town on a modern double-decker coach, seated on the top deck, giving me enticing glimpses of Hong Kong. The city's lights magically exploded into life at dusk. With no pre-booking or any idea of the geography, I was literally in the dark when

I descended from the bus in Wan Chai just to the east of central Hong Kong.

I needed a new plan of action after trudging around for a while with no sign of any budget hotels or guesthouses - although there were plenty of 'top dollar' places. I went into one of these 5-star establishments to seek information, swiftly disavowing the concierge that I was seeking accommodation in their fine establishment. He had guessed that I am sure, as most of their clientele seemed to arrive with matching Louis Vuitton luggage or similar, not a battered rucksack. Anyway, the chap was most helpful, made some enquiries and came up with a place on Wan Chai Road only a few hundred metres from where I was currently standing. I thanked the obliging man and headed off.

The guesthouse was on the 7th floor of a shabby, dark, anonymous tower block. At least the lift worked. On arrival at the reception area, it pleasantly surprised me to find that the place was homely, with just a few rooms for rent, and ideal for my purposes. Run by a friendly, elderly Chinese couple with limited English, we established I required a room for a few nights. We negotiated the rate down to an acceptable $240 Hong Kong or £24 for a small bedroom with a double bed and en suite facilities. It was a fair chunk and I would have liked to have been paying less, but it was around 7.30 pm, so my options were fast disappearing. Hong Kong was understandably more expensive than Indonesia or Thailand, where decent places were available for just a few pounds a night.

In the evening, I explored Wan Chai, being taken in by the sheer pizzazz of the place. Gleaming skyscrapers surrounded me and could see dozens more over on Kowloon on the other side of the dark waters of the magnificent Victoria harbour, glistening in the moonlight.

At ground level, everything was bright neon, and a cacophony of human voices and traffic noise assaulted the ears. Chinese New Year decorations were in place as people hurried about their business or entered one of the many bars for after-work drinks. They had lavishly decorated many buildings with illuminated New Year messages.

On first impressions, I found Hong Kong scruffier, edgier, and noisier than Singapore, but somehow more loveable for that. Ancient wooden trams clattered by, a charming anachronism in the ultra-modern hi-tech city.

I chose a basic and busy restaurant from the many available and was quickly and efficiently served up with a tasty duck breast, pak choi, fried rice and hoisin sauce. A decent beer went down well. Then, after refuelling, I spent a pleasant hour walking around the side streets. Taking in all the wonderful sights, sounds and aromas that the wonderfully eclectic city-state offered, I found it quite magical. Retracing my steps, I then orientated my way back for a relatively early night.

The following day, grabbing a coffee on the run like so many of the locals, I headed down to the Wan Chai ferry pier. I had no particular plan, just to grasp the opportunity to explore this wonderfully atmospheric Pearl of the Orient fully and quickly; it occurred to me that a ferry trip across the iconic harbour was a great place to start.

Like when taking a ferry crossing over Sydney Harbour a few months back, I found myself quite envious of the hordes of commuters for whom that evocative mode of transport was just an everyday occurrence.

The frequent and regular crossings run by Star Ferries cost the equivalent of a few pennies. This makes it exceptional value for money and offers fabulous views of Kowloon, Hong Kong Island and the mountains beyond. It also afforded a close-up examination of the constant and varied commercial shipping in the harbour, as well as traditional red-sailed junks.

Over on the mainland, Kowloon side, I spent half an hour exploring the busy streets before I found myself attracted to the Hong Kong History Museum. Bypassing the geological and prehistoric sections, I hurried on to the displays, giving insight into more modern British colonial times.

In the mid-19th century, I gleaned that there was a tremendous demand from Britain for Chinese tea, porcelain, and silks, which gave rise to a considerable trade imbalance between the two nations. From the British point of view, the solution to this problem was to supply China with vast quantities of opium, which was grown in India and shipped over.

Initially, the Chinese generally consumed opium with tea or water in small amounts with no real ill effects; they perceived the highly addictive drug as a medicine. However, the increasingly popular habit of smoking the product as a recreational drug rapidly led to massive social problems.

Soon there were well over ten million addicts in China - but we Brits had restored the trade balance.

The Chinese authorities were understandably unhappy about what was happening, and tensions grew, leading to the First Opium War of 1840 after Commissioner Lim destroyed British-owned stocks of opium in Canton.

Several military engagements between the adversaries resulted from this unilateral action. The British held the upper hand with superior weaponry and other military technology, though feathers had been well and truly ruffled. Shaken by events, the Chinese Qing government dismissed Lim and dispatched a replacement to negotiate peace. Early discussions came to nought, and hostilities resumed with Guangzhou (Canton) falling to the British.

The Treaty of Nanking followed in 1842, with China ceding Hong Kong to the United Kingdom. Claiming China did not fully honour the Nanking Treaty, the British then engaged in further provocative behaviour as they renewed territorial designs on China. The Second Opium War started in 1859. Finally, the British forced more concessions, formalised in the Treaty of Tientsin.

Then, in 1898, the UK gained control of the New Territories, north of Kowloon, on the mainland. Eventually, the former combatants signed a 99-year lease for the entire region, the expiry of which in 1997 became the fulcrum for Hong Kong's return to China.

Once under British control, they declared Hong Kong a free port, attracting a constant flow of goods, capital investment and enterprise.

The opening up of the Suez Canal in 1869 aided trade with Asia by considerably shortening the sea route from Europe. Hong Kong boomed.

Whilst the city's commercial wealth and influence grew, a shortage of land was always a problem, inhibiting further expansion. Many land reclamation schemes (including for the new airport) had extended the landmass, and construction projects undertaken on the rugged hills above Hong Kong were a testament to the shortage of decent building land. Indeed, they highlighted the local people's enterprise, initiative, and engineering skills in overcoming these natural barriers to development.

The Japanese seized Hong Kong in 1941, and the British surrendered on Christmas Day of that year. As in Singapore, the Japanese brutalised the local population and the three years and eight months of Japanese control caused untold misery and suffering. People lived in terror of a visit from the hated and brutal Kempeitai, the secret military police. In the post-war period, Hong Kong bounced back from the traumatic period of Japanese occupation with commendable resilience.

I had become quite lost in time in my quest to delve into something of the history of Hong Kong. I felt the need to get outside the museum environment into the fresh air and carry on with my exploration of the present-day city.

After a lunchtime snack from a street vendor, I took the ferry back to the island, having decided I wanted to have a look at Happy Valley. I knew this area was primarily an extensive racecourse but had many sporting pitches within its environs. It was a leisure and recreational oasis in the middle of an ultra-commercial world. The place in the photographs I had seen looked dramatic, the former swamp area being about the only sizeable expanse of flat land on the island. Happy Valley is surrounded and over-shadowed by hugely impressive commercial skyscrapers and upmarket apartments.

I walked out to the south of my Wan Chai home territory. Presently, I came across what seemed to be an incongruously vast acreage of green space with an enormous modern grandstand beside the racecourse. There was also a range of commercial and hospitality buildings belonging to the Hong Kong Jockey Club. The place exuded wealth and privilege. It was not unlike Ascot.

In the middle of the track and on the periphery were large numbers of grass and multipurpose all-weather pitches and courts for a wide range of community and club sports. The place was thronging with runners, joggers, cyclists and soccer, hockey, tennis and rugby players, practising their particular specialisms or playing competitive matches. It was hectic because it was a Saturday afternoon.

The Hong Kong Jockey Club, which runs Happy Valley, was a not-for-profit organisation that had existed since the late nineteenth century. It seemed most commendable that the authorities had enabled such a massive chunk of prime real estate, in a region commanding some of the world's highest property prices, to be made available for sport and community recreation.

Seeing some rugby guys in action made me think I needed to find somewhere to watch the England v Ireland game on television later on. Dining early, I then returned to my home base, searching for somewhere that would show the match.

Delaney's, a large and rambling faux Irish place in Wan Chai, fitted the bill. Wan Chai, it seemed to me, was a pretty good district that had the lot.

After I had bought a beer, I Slotted in easily with a friendly ex-pat crowd. They were enjoying a couple of anticipatory beers before the England game kicked off. Hopefully, it would be a better performance than the last time out against the Scots. A couple of weeks earlier, the win had been less than convincing.

I thought back to the last England match I'd seen against the Irish. It was a Six Nations game played after a lengthy delay in the autumn, rather than spring, because of the foot and mouth outbreak in the UK. I'd watched in Chiang Mai with Irish and Kiwis friends. They enjoyed some delicious schadenfreude at my expense as they took us to the cleaners, denying us our Grand Slam hopes.

What I was delighted to witness when the game finally got underway was a sublime performance from England, who played the best rugby I had ever seen from them. I think the Irish were a little shell-shocked as the men in white rampaged around the pitch. In the last twenty minutes of the first half and the first twenty of the second, they scored six converted and unanswered tries. Everything during that period worked so well; they were a well-oiled machine; the backs ripping through the Irish defences at will after the forwards had delivered a stream of fast, front-foot ball for playmaker Jonny Wilkinson to weave his magic. It was as if I was watching the Hong Kong Sevens rather than the Six Nations; such was the incisive skill and pace on show from the back line.

I had a few celebratory drinks with my new friends and tried to watch the Wales v France game where I would have appreciated the Taffs downing the French. We had to play the latter away from home later in the tournament. The French won a close game 37-33, but I could not focus on the match properly, being heavily involved in après match beer and banter.

On the Sunday I enjoyed a bit of a lie-in after my new party friends had kept me up beyond 4 am. Once up, I decided I should move from my modest hotel over to Kowloon, where I had seen hostel accommodation was available for a quarter of what I was currently paying.

I took one of the ancient wooden trams down to the ferry port and headed over to the harbour, savouring the views and the experience. The place I found in Kowloon was again halfway up a tower block, clean and modern, if a little tight for space. I was not over pleased to be experiencing dormitory accommodation for the first time in Australia some months previously. SE Asia had spoiled me by being able to find decent-sized private rooms with full facilities for just a few pounds a night. It made budget sense to make the move, though.

Having cleared the formalities at reception and dumped my bag on the allotted bunk, I ventured out to see more of the Kowloon side of Hong Kong. I soon found the impressive Kowloon Park, which was very popular with young couples and extended families enjoying a walk in the fresh air on that bright Sunday morning. It reminded me of strolling through a park in Darling Harbour in Sydney on the Sunday after the third and deciding Lions' test the previous July.

This time my immediate rugby memories were far more positive. It delighted me when I reflected on the way we put the Irish to the sword just a few hours previously. The thoughts from Sydney were more 'what ifs' and 'should haves' as we threw away an excellent opportunity for a series win.

I came out of the park and headed back down to the waterfront, where I had in mind to investigate the iconic Peninsula Hotel, one of the world's premier hotels.

The Peninsula, built in a colonial style and opened in 1928, was grand and opulent. With a five-star accreditation, the establishment was renowned as a place for the rich and famous to see and be seen. Particularly at its peak in the thirties, with daily afternoon tea dances, dinner soirees and regular concerts. The Peninsula also became popular with the entire community.

In the city state's darkest times, the hotel became the HQ for the Japanese administration. The occupying forces even took the formal British surrender in their sumptuous third-floor suites on Christmas Day 1941.

I wandered in, passing the courteously bowing and finely liveried doorman, and strolled around in the plush and extensive lobby area, a string quartet playing beautifully in the corner. I possibly gave the impression that I was about to take tea. In reality, I just wanted to savour some of the undoubted atmosphere and imagine the place in its early days when I might have bumped into Charlie Chaplin in the lobby.

Michael Palin visited the Peninsula on his acclaimed *Around the World in Eighty Days* expedition, but I am not sure he stayed. He was probably in a backpacker hostel down the road like I was. It was all rather lovely as I strolled down the fashion arcade featuring high-end baubles from the likes of Tiffany, Gucci, Chanel and Dior.

Back to reality, I left the Peninsula and walked along to the increasingly familiar Star Ferry embarkation point before crossing the harbour again.

The city was bustling in the Central District. Many people (women mainly) were practising competitive retail therapy, hurrying from big-name store to store festooned with branded carrier bags filled with clothing, shoes, and cosmetics. It was the New Year sales time.

I later took the world's longest escalator up to Mid Station, the halfway station for the funicular up to the Peak. This was an area of even more shops and restaurants and an exclusive residential district. I would have gone up higher, but the weather had clouded over, meaning there would not be any sort of view from the lookout point. So I walked back down through various market areas specialising in meat, fish or fruit and vegetables and even insects.

Whilst the very concept of eating insects is anathema to Westerners, two billion people a day regularly eat bugs. Fried, boiled, sauteed, roasted or baked with a bit of oil and some salt.

Full of protein and highly nutritious - lovely. Insects will probably become a worldwide source of protein in the future.

They also featured insects prominently in the Asian sporting world; specialists bred thoroughbred male crickets for fighting. I saw some impressive examples being offered for sale by some unsavoury characters outside the principal markets.

Bouts draw crowds of enthusiastic punters who gamble illicitly and enthusiastically on the outcomes in Hong Kong and throughout China and other parts of SE Asia. They cosset their highly prized top performers of the entomological world. They feed them a high-protein diet and even have a female cricket popped into their accommodation before a contest, which gets their hormones fizzing and improves their fighting abilities.

Eventually, I got down to sea level and took the ferry back over to Kowloon. I had walked a fair distance, discovered more of Hong Kong, checked out the Peninsula and crossed the harbour twice. It was now time for a sit-down, a beer, and some food. There were plenty of choices for spending a relaxing hour or two, which fitted the bill nicely.

I wanted to make it up to the Peak at some stage of my stay in Hong Kong and enjoy a bird's-eye view of the city and the harbour. However, the next day dawned very misty, so this would not be workable immediately. Instead, I allowed myself to be seduced by the delicious aromas emerging from a busy little noodle shop across the road and considered my options as I enjoyed some breakfast.

As I was soon about to venture into China, I concluded I needed to get a guidebook; I knew I could get one over on the other side of the harbour. My *South East Asia on a Shoestring* did not cover China, and as I knew very little about the geography of the country felt this would be a beneficial acquisition. So, this would be task number one for the day.

I took the increasingly familiar ferry and was soon the proud owner of a new edition of Lonely Planet's *South-West China*. The new guidebook would be essential, as I didn't know where I wanted to go and what to explore in the world's most populous country. China was so vast - the third or fourth-largest country in the world by area - but to me, a massive unknown.

I had decided that going overland up to Beijing and the north and east of the country seemed a little ambitious, so I decided I would focus on the SW of China.

On a whim, after my brief shopping trip, I took a bus out to Stanley, a popular beach resort area, to get away from Hong Kong's humming centre for a while. The gleaming new double-decker took me past Happy Valley and beyond the Hong Kong Tennis Centre and the Hong Kong Cricket Club. This club involved bats, balls and flannelled fools rather than gladiators of the insect world, I believe. Both sports clubs looked to be highly affluent establishments with top-notch facilities. We followed the sinuous road up and over the steep, rugged hills, where towering apartment blocks clung precariously to seemingly precipitous slopes. As the early mist disappeared and the sun shone, the trip afforded fabulous views back over the harbour.

Once in Stanley, named after Lord Stanley, the British colonial secretary at the time of the ceding of Hong Kong from the Chinese to Britain, I walked along the promenade. This walkway flanked a lovely beach with many evocative bars and restaurants on the landward side of the road. The sea looked quite inviting, but I noticed they had netted it to prevent predatory sharks from gaining access.

At the end of the beach, I climbed up some steep steps and dropped onto a second beach before hopping on a convenient bus bound for Causeway Bay. I continued my exploration of Hong Kong island's hinterland. Once around Repulse Bay, the bus, rather than climbing over the mountainous terrain, took a long tunnel, and it surprised me when we emerged into the central business district again.

With the weather having improved and good visibility in prospect, I ventured up to the 400m high Victoria Peak. I walked across Wan Chai, up through the delightful Chater Garden and past the Legislative Council Chamber and Exchange Square. Walking along to Lan Kwai Fong, usually abbreviated by the locals as LKF, a trendy ex-pat club, bar and dining district, I took a break in the warm sunshine.

I found a suitable place to sit for a brief while before heading to the nearby Mid-station and this time completing the journey to the Peak via the ancient funicular railway.

It was touristy at the top with souvenir stalls and such, but nothing could detract from the outstanding panoramic views over the city, the harbour, Kowloon, and mainland China beyond. Breathtaking.

After spending a little time to do the views justice, I made my way back down towards the Central District on foot. Walking down from Victoria Peak, I reflected I had made a reasonably comprehensive exploration of Hong Kong over the past couple of days. However, I had not seen one of the city sights that was etched in my mind from my very young days. That of junks, dragon boats and garishly coloured and illuminated floating restaurants. I had established that the place I was thinking of was Aberdeen Harbour and decided that I would go there for my evening meal.

I worked out which bus I needed and took the twenty-minute journey out to Aberdeen as dusk fell. As we descended into the moonlit bay, I saw the gigantic and quite garish Jumbo floating restaurant in mid-harbour. Bright scarlet and with lots of gold flourishes, fully illuminated with hundreds of yellow lights and with massive green lettering spelling out Jumbo, it was certainly not hiding its light under a bushel. They based the design on the style of an ancient imperial palace. Jumbo was where I was going to dine.

I got off the bus and found a seafront hostelry, which I thought would be ideal for an apéritif, as it was a little early for dinner. Moments earlier, I had ventured into a place thinking it was a bar and raised many inscrutable oriental eyebrows as I disturbed a mah-jong competition of some sort.

Looking out at the harbour from my window seat, once I had finally found a suitable bar, I could see that Aberdeen still boasted a sizeable traditional fishing fleet at anchor. Further around was a goodly collection of gleaming white gin palaces, presumably owned by the region's wealthy business executives and successful entrepreneurs, bobbing at anchor.

The next consideration was how I could get out to the restaurant; but then I noticed a succession of little wooden craft plying the route from the promenade over to Jumbo. A water taxi would be the answer.

I spoke with the skipper of one of these small, sleek mahogany vessels, finished magnificently with beautiful brass fittings. It was the owner's pride and joy. They laid on this free shuttle service for diners, which was great news.

We motored over in sedate fashion, and one of the many elegantly uniformed staff greeted me on arrival and helped me ashore.

Billed as the world's most luxurious floating restaurant, it certainly lived up to that appellation. There were marble walls, sumptuous tiling, deep piled carpets, artwork on the walls, lots of statues, vibrant plants and flowers, red and gold dragons and decorative lanterns in abundance. There were also many framed and signed photographs of prominent visitors. The effect on the senses was one of over-the-top chinoiserie.

A server ushered me into the main restaurant hall (I believe there were some other smaller, more exclusive dining rooms) and found (sadly) a table for one.

The place was three-quarters full of couples and larger groups of extended families and friends.

I perused the menu. The shark's fin soup on page one was a snip at £52. I needed to be a little cautious if I were not to destroy my budgeting plans. I chose a duck and noodle dish and ordered a beer that was not too excessive.

The food was excellent but perhaps secondary to the experience of dining whilst floating in the middle of Aberdeen Harbour, Hong Kong. Previous diners at Jumbo had included our own Queen, John Wayne, David Bowie, Tom Cruise and Gwyneth Paltrow, amongst scores of others.

I savoured the moment, taking my time over a second drink before being ferried back to dry land and getting a taxi back home. It was a memorable, brief interlude and a fitting time to end my visit to Hong Kong.

Chapter 6

MACAU A TASTE OF PORTUGAL IN THE ORIENT

The next day, I picked up my newly visa-d passport and walked round to the ferry terminal. I admired the hugely impressive *Star Princess* cruise liner lying at berth and passed several ferries destined for various Chinese ports. Further along the front, I found the sleek modern vessel that would take me to Macau. The fast ferry with aircraft-style seating in the main saloon would complete the trip in an hour.

I had an excellent window seat, which was initially fine as we slowly left the harbour. However, once we geared up to top speed, I could only see the vast amounts of spray being kicked up. I noticed many of the Chinese on board were avidly reading glossy brochures from the many casino-hotels in Macau. It was quite obvious where they would head on arrival at the port city.

Macau, which I had thought to be an island, was in reality on a peninsula and part of the Chinese mainland on the Pearl River estuary.

The authorities in China controlled gambling tightly. They did not allow it on the mainland (except in Macau), and even in Hong Kong, they kept the industry under strict control. The Hong Kong Jockey Club held a monopoly for gambling on horse races under stringent rules.

Macau, the Portuguese's first European outpost in the Far East and settled in the sixteenth century, had been a gambling mecca for many years. There were now dozens of huge flashy casinos, and while the city was since December 1999, back under direct Chinese control, there had been no move to put a stop to the industry. The Monte Carlo of Asia was generating 40% of its GDP from gambling. In an English language local paper, I also read that some Las Vegas mogul was looking to invest $4 US billion into the Macau gambling and hotel industry shortly. The authorities appeared to take a pragmatic view of the development of this highly lucrative business.

I had visited one SAR or Special Administrative Region in Hong Kong. I was now entering another, so on arrival in Macau had to go through the usual passport and immigration controls. Officials made only a cursory inspection of my shabby passport and new visa and waved me on through.

After calling briefly at a convenient information desk to pick up a map and other helpful literature, I hopped straight on to the waiting number 3 bus for a brief ride into town. Scooters seemed to be the personal transportation of choice, and thousands of them were weaving in and out of the trucks and buses. Most were being ridden cautiously and at moderate speeds, reminiscent of what I had observed in Hanoi and Ho Chi Min City some months earlier.

I had asked about budget accommodation and, having been told there was a good choice in the centre of town, I quickly found Rua da Felicidade. This thoroughfare was a lively street with hawkers selling a range of snacks, including nougat cookies and the local take on the Portuguese staple of *'pastas de nata'* (custard tarts). Behind the stalls were many Chinese pharmacies and medicinal teashops. In addition, there were several guesthouses and cheaper hotels.

Much smaller than Hong Kong, with a population of around

400,000 as opposed to Hong Kong's six million, I had already realised that the city had kept much more of its old colonial charm, at least in the central area. The familiar (for anyone who has visited Portugal) black-and-white mosaic paving was highly evocative of the western Iberian Peninsula.

I tried one small hotel, and the proprietor showed me a lovely room for about a third of what I would have had to pay in Hong Kong. It was available for $110 HK. It was the first place I had tried, and it was still quite early. I explored the area a little further.

At a small crossroads, and after being persuaded by an enthusiastic stallholder to try a few freebie titbits, I spotted an elegant terrace of lovely old Sino-Portuguese properties. These lovely buildings boasted wrought iron canopies, elaborate balconies, and dark green painted wooden shutters.

The first property announced itself to be San Va Hospedaria, or in Portuguese, a hostel. I had a look. It was a delightful place, oozing with charm and available for $70 (about £7 a night). The lady in charge offered me a spacious, dark wooden floored double room with a high ceiling, complete with a fan and a wide, full-height window. There was also a small balcony overlooking the bustling street scene below. A large old double bed, with a substantial fat mattress and thick duvet, looked quite irresistible. Other furniture items were of a certain vintage but perfectly serviceable, and there was even a washbasin and jug and a chamber pot under the bed. It was perfect. I told her I would take it.

That the shower and loo were on the floor above did not matter. The accommodation was something authentic and several notches above a cramped dorm in Kowloon. It was also so well located in terms of proximity to the city centre. I discarded my rucksack immediately and was soon out exploring.

Navigating the narrow lane opposite, crammed with more sweetmeat stalls, I circled back onto the main Avenida Almeida Ribeiro. I walked on down towards the harbour area, past a lot of dried fish stalls giving off a distinctive pungent odour, and watched a chap on a live fish stall. He was having a bit of a battle with a giant and recalcitrant lobster that he was trying to weigh for a customer.

Suddenly realising I needed to get some local cash, I doubled back, saving an exploration of the harbour for later. I soon came across the Largo do Senado, a central piazza area with a large fountain displaying gold and red Chinese New Year signage and other paraphernalia. The latter was the only thing that persuaded me I was still in the Orient. Everything else seemed pure Portugal, particularly the vast expanse of swirling black and white mosaic block work on the floor. There were also fine examples of the blue-on-white ceramic tiled street names and *'azulejos'* (blue decorative tiling) on several walls.

I found somewhere to get some cash and continued my exploration. I dived off down a couple of side streets so narrow that neighbours could have shaken hands across the street from the first-floor bedroom windows. Peeling pastel paintwork, multiple potted plants and washing festooned on lines running from balconies reminded me of the Alfama district in Lisbon. I liked the old town of Macau.

Round the corner, the neo-classical Cathedral of the Nativity of our Lady of Macau confronted me. This attractive building, looking exquisite in a buttery pale cream plaster finish and with substantial dark green doors. I could almost imagine early colonists walking to services in their Sunday best.

I strolled on, and around another turn, it surprised me to see the elegant ruins of St Paul's church. Fire destroyed the bulk of the building in 1835, leaving just a majestic façade at the top of a series of wide stone steps. I walked up to have a good look at the remains and back over the city from the high vantage point it afforded. Macau was undoubtedly throwing up some treasures.

Walking further afield, I came to the vast, modern Grand Hotel Lisboa, a forty-seven-floor edifice. A garishly, kitschy monstrosity of a hotel and casino complex in the centre of the luxury accommodation and gambling district. Fascinated by its sheer vulgarity, I stepped inside. I saw the hundreds of dead-eyed gamblers from Hong Kong and mainland China doing whatever they do, sitting at green baize tables. Or else in front of banks of clanking, whirring and flashing machines. I didn't stay long.

The area seemed to be all about money and wealth, and there were innumerable jewellers in the vicinity with unbelievably extensive arrays of gold on display. Most of these establishments appeared to have no customers. But up to a dozen completely idle staff twiddling their thumbs, looking terminally bored and with blank expressions on their faces. Armed Security guards sat at the entrances, toying with their automatic weapons. Ahead of me, I could see more hotels and casinos, but had seen enough and headed back into the old town. Once there, I found an authentic and atmospheric little place for some food and a beer. I then headed back to my new base to read and relax for a while.

The next day would be my only full day in Macau. As well as sorting out the logistics of my transportation into mainland China, I wanted to discover more of this colonial gem.

I started in the morning by heading down to the fishing harbour, the Doca dos Pescadores. The fishing industry here had declined over the last few decades, but there was plenty of activity on the water and at the harbourside. Onshore, many of the fishing community were mending nets, and men and women were industriously filleting and pegging out hundreds of fish to dry in readiness for sale. The Doca was a working-class part of town and dilapidated tenement buildings lining the shore road had full-height security grilles on balconies. It did not seem to be the sort of place to venture out after dark.

It was a warm sunny day, and at that moment, I was happy to sit and watch the port activity and feel the sun on my back. I settled down outside a pavement café with a coffee and spent a pleasant half-hour watching the nautical world go by. The water traffic included a couple of beautifully refurbished wooden junks full of Chinese tourists that were crisscrossing the harbour on pleasure cruises.

Later I found a bus information place where I deciphered where I should catch a bus to Guangzhou (formerly known as Canton) and begin my exploration of SW China. I didn't get anywhere, though, to establish the timings of such departures. I decided just to turn up in the morning and see what happened.

My further explorations took me to a large and impressive Moorish-style house built in the early 1900s, known as the Sun Yat-Sen Memorial House. This place was now a museum dedicated to the memory of the founder of modern China and, in 1912, its first president. I knew his name from my stamp collecting days as a boy, as his visage appeared on countless Chinese stamps from that period. There were some difficult periods in Sun Yat-sen's career, and at one time, he stayed in Macau in hiding from his many enemies. His wife died at the house in 1952.

Later, I happened upon the delightful Jardim Lou Lim Leoc, formerly a private garden but later donated to the city and enjoyed as a beautiful tranquil park by the grateful populace. The gardens were conveniently situated close to the middle of town. I enjoyed strolling around for a while, admiring the planting and the sculptures. Finding a bench with a sunny aspect, I decided it would be an ideal place to sit down to give my legs a bit of a break. Back at my hostel for a shower and freshen up, I came out later to enjoy a final relaxed evening over a leisurely meal with my book for company.

Early in the morning, I walked to the Kee Kwan bus depot about which I had been told. I tried to get a ticket from the kiosk, but the lady behind the screen just repeated

"Eight o'clock."

to any question I asked.

It was about twenty minutes to the hour, so I wandered about as the city woke up to the working day.

A small group of older people were out practising their Tai Chi exercise routines at the side of the road. I watched a tallyman checking out vast amounts of beautifully coloured blooms. These had just been purchased by retailers from the wholesale flower market. Loading them into their pickups and chatting animatedly and incessantly, the florists, mainly women, enthusiastically went about their business. They were seemingly more than content with their lot. Some women carried the flowers on double panniers suspended from yokes Vietnamese style and were tottering off down the road. One woman, the joker in the pack, caught my eye and gestured for me to have a go, carrying her heavy burden. Cue much cackling amusement from her friends as I struggled with the load. I certainly would not have liked to go far with such a burden.

Chapter 7

THE REAL CHINA

As it was now 8 am, the lady at the kiosk deigned to sell me a ticket. It certainly did not offer me much information, just a thin, photocopied piece of paper covered in Chinese characters. However, going with the flow, when a battered bus duly arrived, I raced over with a score of others. Everyone else was heavily laden with overfilled, cheap, woven plastic bags and other tatty luggage. This vehicle took me a short distance to Gongbei port, where we all disembarked to approach customs and immigration. We negotiated the formalities smoothly, although a junior official, a spotty adolescent jobsworth in an oversized uniform, took it upon himself to refer my poor passport to a higher authority. The senior officer, who he summoned, could thankfully give the document his seal of approval. I smiled in gratitude at both the man and the ambitious lad. *Can't be too careful with petty bureaucrats*, was my thinking.

Transferred to a modern and comfortable coach, we continued our three-hour journey, travelling through a flat, rich and intensively cultivated alluvial plain, part of the Pearl River delta. The time passed pleasantly enough, though I could have done without the freezing air conditioning and the Chinese opera blaring out of several television screens.

We finally came to a halt at the upmarket China Hotel somewhere in downtown Guangzhou, and we all trudged off the coach. People dispersed rapidly in all directions on foot or piled into waiting taxis or private cars. I went into the hotel to get a tourist map and set out for the train and adjacent bus station a few blocks away.

I had absolutely no plan in mind.

In front of the railway station, the piazza area was a heaving mass of humanity sitting around on their battered and shabby luggage. They were eating noodles, chatting or curling up trying to sleep. There were departure boards on the front of the station building, but no information in English. It was not possible to get into the station without a ticket, and there were huge queues for the ticket kiosks. However, for me, there was no way of working out what journeys were possible and at what times.

Next step I thought would be to try the bus station next door.

Same story there. Masses of people, no information available in English. I was getting a little frustrated. It was pointless asking anyone, as no one appeared to speak English.

It was after lunchtime, and I decided I would stay the night, so the next task was to find some accommodation. I looked around for a suitable hotel or guesthouse, and eventually, I found a suitable down-at-heel place that would suit my requirements. The room cost a reasonable 100Y.

I congratulated myself on finding a refuge where I could plan my future strategy. The room, spacious with a decent western loo and shower and a colossal television, was eminently suitable.

I enjoyed a good long shower, which helped to ease the tiredness I felt from my early start and the day of travelling. Nicely refreshed, I retraced my steps to the bus station, deciding that coach travel appeared easier to organise.

Before reaching the terminus, I popped into a smart hotel to see if they had any travel information in English. They didn't, but I struck lucky in that they had a bright junior assistant manager who was keen to practise his more than passable English and help me out.

The Real China

He enthusiastically phoned the bus depot to confirm the availability of coaches to Wuzhou. Neatly writing out all the relevant details in English and Chinese for me to hand over at the ticket office, he gave me a piece of paper with a smile and a little bow.

An hour later, I had a ticket in my hand for the next morning's departure and was having supper at an excellent little food court I had discovered locally. A decent pint of beer, which cost the equivalent of 50p, accompanied the food. Things were looking up.

The city, a sprawling place of, conservatively, some ten million souls, would have been difficult to explore on foot, so I took a taxi out to have a look at the Pearl River area. It dropped me at the Swan hotel, an impressive four or five-star affair, but I hastened on to explore the elegant waterside avenue.

The area was on an island in the middle of the broad brown river and was once under British and then later French control. Some beautiful old buildings reflected this colonial influence.

I had a drink in the Garden Bar where families of moneyed middle-class Chinese were dining. Customers were barbequing a selection of fish and meat on rickety tabletop charcoal grills.

After finishing my drink, I walked on, past a smart local tennis club where some talented youngsters were in action, over a bridge to the other side of the river. Moored here were some brightly illuminated Pearl River cruising boats, regularly departing with full loads of Chinese tourists, taking in the sights and enjoying an evening trip.

I walked on a little more beyond the wharf area and took the promenade for a while. It all seemed a little low-key, so I returned to an area where I could hail a taxi and return home.

The following day I was back at the bus station in good time to travel on to Wuzhou. It was busy, and there was a veritable army of ostentatiously uniformed adolescents on crowd control duties. They brandished their swagger sticks like parade ground sergeant majors trying to herd people into the right areas.

I found the right vehicle and settled down for the five-and-a-half-hour journey in a wide and comfortable window seat without being hassled.

Traffic was light, although it appeared we were taking new toll roads frequently, which was probably not the way many locals travelled. We passed through areas of intensive market gardening and scores of paddy fields and orchards. Small villages with ramshackle brick-built houses dotted the route. The main road bypassed larger industrial towns with soot-blackened factories belching out billowing plumes of dark grey smoke.

Crossing rivers frequently, I noticed a lot of commercial activity on the wide watercourses. Stopping for refuelling and a bit of a break at one stage, I counted seven uniformed petrol pump attendants hanging around, with our coach the only vehicle needing fuel.

My *Lonely Planet* had told me the journey would take over five hours, but we arrived comfortably in four, which was a pleasant surprise. Road improvements had worked to reduce journey times considerably.

Wuzhou bus station was ideally in the centre of the city. I found a room at the nearby Labour Union Hotel for a 30% lower rate than in Guangzhou.

I was hungry, so after I had checked in and dumped my bag in the more than adequate, if old-fashioned, large double room, I headed out to find somewhere for a spot of lunch. A basic chicken stir-fry and rice at an unassuming small worker's café fitted the bill.

Afterwards, I wandered about to discover what the city offered. While a bit run down, grey, drab and careworn, it was not without a certain charm. Hundreds of bicycles filled the streets; locals sedately cycled by, tinkling their bells on ancient old 'sit up and beg' bicycles. Many had been shopping at the dozens of market stalls skirting the road, with panniers stuffed with fresh produce.

Shabby canvas-covered market stalls were everywhere and doing good business. There were the typical fruit and vegetable places, butchers with their disgusting-looking bloody offerings of indeterminate provenance, leather goods, tailors, scores of clothing places offering cheap trousers and tee-shirts and toy stalls attracting interest from raggedy bare-bottomed toddlers.

I found a large pedestrianised street with even more stalls and shops and then suddenly I came face to face with an emu. Thinking that coming across a sizeable flightless Australian bird in this location was a little strange, I undertook some further investigation. I soon realised I was on the ground floor of a restaurant. There were two glass-sided rooms at either side of a corridor leading through to the stairs to the first-floor restaurant. This was the menu.

The emu was by far the biggest creature on his side of the place, sharing space with quail, ducks, geese, doves and other assorted game birds. The room on the other side had a choice of snakes, frogs, turtles, tortoises and cats, as well as a tank full of weird and wonderful fish. It was quite an extensive bill of fare, but I gave the place a miss.

Further down, at a little tree-shaded square, highly competitive games of mah-jong, dominoes, chess and cards engrossed groups of old men. All the games seemed to involve the loud slamming down of tiles, chess pieces or playing cards. In another part of the piazza, the activity of choice involved many middle-aged men trading coins, stamps and medals.

For other men, standing in clumps on street corners, competitive smoking and spitting kept them busy. Expectoration was, I had noticed in my brief time in China, considered a particular art form. Men were the major participants, but they did not have a monopoly, as I had observed several highly talented female performers. Gobbing up enormous balls of phlegm from deep inside their lungs and then projecting the resultant globules at walls, floors and items of furniture required considerable skill and hours of practice.

I stopped for a coffee and plumped for the western-orientated Monte Carlo. Here there were seven front-of-house staff and a cashier on duty - and no customers. The bored-looking cashier sat at her station fiddling with her phone; other staff crowded around a blaring television, three of them asleep, heads in arms at the table. I got a drink in the end.

I walked down to the river, where I found a row of sadly unkempt restaurants with broken windows and peeling paintwork. They all seemed open for business, but they did not look at all inviting.

By now, it was early evening, and I walked back to my base. On a whim, I went into a garishly lit place pertaining to a bar and disco, according to the neon signage.

About a dozen staff welcomed me in. Four young women 'greeters' were in full-length gold lame ball gowns as last seen on *Come Dancing* circa 1965. One girl boldly stepped forward, obviously the English speaker, and welcomed me effusively, clasping both my hands.

I said that I just wanted a beer, and she escorted me upstairs to the VIP lounge., Half a dozen more females promoting their own particular brand of beer accosted me. I chose one, and away they went.

Through the dry ice and flashing lights, I saw a young lady coming out onto the stage who sang, competently, I might add, three Bette Midler songs in a row. Still no beer. The girl behind the bar just looked around distractedly, as did the battalion of uniformed security men/floor managers.

The place filled up a little with young men in shiny best suits as worn by Albert Finney and Tom Courtenay in mid-sixties northern films about the travails of the working classes. Other young men followed and strutted about, seemingly members of the Red Army (Youth Section), all gold braid and peaked caps. Still, nobody seemed to have a drink.

I had had enough.

I met my greeter at the entrance on the way out, and she thanked me again profusely for coming. *A pleasure,* I thought.

I now really needed a nice cold beer. I tried one place, but all they could offer was a dusty lukewarm can, so I had to resort to the piano bar at a smart hotel down the road. It was a place I would normally avoid, but here, it proved to be a little oasis of sanity.

Moving on a bit later, I saw another neon-lit 'disco', and the music I could hear through the open doors was decent western pop and rock. I ventured into the place and immersed myself completely in the Wuzhou entertainment scene.

This place was quite busy; everyone was friendly and keen to show their linguistic skills, and the well-turned-out serving staff brought me a drink quickly. They offered me one drink for 15 RMB or six for 50 RMB, so for me, it was a straightforward choice. This place was indeed a notch up on my first Wuzhou disco experience, and I spent the rest of my evening there enjoyably.

Up early the next morning, I went to the bus station, bought a ticket, and was told I needed to take a free shuttle bus ride. The newer bus station, over the river, was where coaches left for Yangzhou. It was a drab, grey and drizzling morning, which matched the monochrome appearance of Hexi, as they called this recently developed district.

I asked around and found my coach, took my comfortable seat and settled down for what I projected to be a seven-hour trip.

I had decided I would head westwards to the region I had read offered more for travellers. For example, superb limestone karst scenery offering trekking and mountain biking opportunities. There were soaring and rugged mountainous areas stretching upward to the Himalayas, and also promises of deep, spectacular gorges, powerful fast-flowing rivers and pretty backpacker-friendly villages.

South West China also boasted a wonderful mix of ethnic minority tribes. Despite all the efforts of the central government to create an homogeneous 'Hanified' populace, sizeable minorities in this region still wore their traditional embroidered homemade clothing. They had their centuries-old customs, feast days and markets and lived their lives in the way they had for generations.

While people of Han ethnicity made up 92% of the Chinese population overall, in SW China, 37% of the population comprised ethnic minority tribes. So it was a considerably different cultural and human melting pot from the more urbanised and developed Mao-suited Han-dominated east of the country.

We were making decent time, and the roads were in good condition, but the steep mountainous terrain and a series of hairpin bends slowed progress. The day was depressingly grey and overcast and matched the drab little settlements we passed through where not a lot seemed to happen. The villages appeared to comprise groups of old men or old women sitting outside chatting morosely.

After one mountainous section, we progressed more rapidly as we sped across a fertile plain where rice and a wide range of vegetables were being grown.

We stopped for some lunch at a windblown, god-forsaken remote service station. The toilet area was disgusting, and I am not the fussiest person about such things.

They provided lunch as part of the ticket price. The offering was primarily gristle, boiled indistinguishable greens and some rice in a tinfoil tray. They dolloped it out like in a prison movie, but if they imposed this sort of effort on prisoners, it would have sparked an instant riot.

We arrived in Yangzhou mid-afternoon. I had already been well and truly wowed by the spectacular, soaring, misshapen limestone pillars, so typical of karst scenery, arising out of the surrounding landscape. The fast-flowing and elegant Lijiang River, commonly known as the Li, also looked spectacular. I couldn't wait to check the area out more fully. It all looked wonderful.

The coach, which was travelling beyond Yangzhou, had stopped on Panto Lu, the main road, right outside a small hotel by the entrance to Xi Jie street. The latter was commonly known as West Street or Foreigner Street. This was a pedestrianised thoroughfare popular with, and catering for, western backpackers.

A lady who introduced herself as Leow came up to me, all smiles and enthusiasm as I got down from the coach. She persuaded me to have a look at her hotel. It seemed as good an idea as any. Within a few minutes, I settled into my pleasant little room in the middle of all the action.

Wasting no time, I was soon out to explore my new surroundings. West Street and Yangzhou had certainly embraced western tourism with considerable enthusiasm. There were many backpacker-orientated cafes, bars, sports equipment and hire shops, souvenir stalls, restaurants and guesthouses. Tour guides or people trying to sell souvenirs or snacks pestered me a little but were not too pushy, as they can be in other parts of SE Asia. I completely fell for the place's charms.

I strolled around the two main pedestrianised streets and then walked down a narrow side path to the more local end of town. Here I found rows of market stalls and an open-air food court selling every conceivable boiled, sauteed or barbequed kind of meat. I even came across a fried rat complete with feet, head and tail being prepared for lunch.

The locals were all smiling and friendly, and the little kids looked up curiously at me as they chewed on sticks of sugar cane, some venturing a shy hello.

It was obviously low season as there were relatively few tourists and travellers about, and I circled and came back onto the main street. I decided where I should eat, having eschewed the fried rat option.

With only limited trade, it must have been a struggle for some restaurants, but for me, it meant a wide choice at very reasonable prices. I found a comfortable place and had a beer at a window table whilst I read for a while before having a king prawn foo yung.

The following day, I was out and about looking for somewhere to hire a mountain bike when I heard someone shout my name. It was Rose, a tour guide I had spoken with the previous evening. She was very keen to take me out cycling around the local area, including taking me to her home village.

"Let's have a coffee and a chat then," I said.

"Ok, over there?" she replied, pointing to a pleasant-looking café on the other side of the street.

Ralph, a twenty-something business consultant, a French national born in Tahiti of part-Chinese lineage, and Simon, a Chinese science graduate from the Beijing University of a similar age, suddenly materialised. Rose had obviously collared the two guys earlier. They had agreed to go out for the day and had hired their bikes. I said I would come along; we decided on the price, and I slipped out to get myself some transport. I struck lucky and found a place that could let me have a brand new machine, and we were soon on our way down to the river Li.

At the riverside, I first saw the cormorant fishermen for which the area was renowned. These chaps had tamed and trained their birds as their companions and assistants to fish for them. Using narrow bamboo skiffs and poling the river bottom for propulsion, they sought the likely spots for fishing success. They tethered the cormorants on a long line and had a constriction device placed around their neck, preventing the bird from swallowing fish. The fisherman would send it down into the waters. After a few moments, the bird duly came up with a fish, which the owner removed, throwing the catch into a basket, and then the process started again.

The birds appear happy enough with the situation; the owner removed the constricting device every so often, and the cormorant was free to catch itself a snack or their master would even feed them smaller fish from the basket. They looked after the cormorants by not having them fish every day, so it seemed a genuinely symbiotic relationship if perhaps slanted in favour of the fisherfolk.

Cormorant fishing in this manner is centuries old, although numbers practising the ancient methods are now diminishing.

We took the bridge across and were soon in a beautiful rural landscape of dirt tracks and a forest of spectacular towering limestone towers. The ubiquitous single-cylinder diesel-engine CRV (Chinese rural vehicle) farm tractors and trailers were the only traffic.

Cycling on through a couple of hamlets, little children enjoyed chasing after us 'helloing' all the time. I chatted with Rose, who told me a bit about herself, the other two being content with their own company.

She was the youngest of three daughters, and her local village had somewhat ostracised her family for not having produced a son. She was thirty-four and her relatives all felt she should have chosen a husband by this stage of her life. But she was strong-willed and determined to plough her own furrow, not feeling ready to take such a step. She had left home to live with her aunt in town and earn a living as a tour guide.

"I do not want to be married yet!" she told me.

"That can wait for a while."

Her family was relatively prosperous at one time, she explained. But circumstances had changed because of some family issues that she seemed unwilling to expand upon. They were now just poor subsistence farmers, her father working on his own and supplementing their income by renting out a couple of fields.

After an hour, we came to Rose's family's house on the edge of a village. It was an ancient, probably three hundred years old, substantial two-storey brick building with an inner courtyard. There was also an open outdoor kitchen area with a lean-to roof.

Her mother welcomed us, gesturing for us to sit down and came out with a hefty lemon-like fruit for our refreshment. In English, Rose told me it was a pomelo and about the size of a coconut. When she removed the thick pithy skin, it tasted like a cross between an orange and a lemon.

After our brief break, we headed on, Rose continuing to give us the names of the various lofty limestone outcrops. We had been told of several from the start of the trip. Antenna Hill was rising high above the city, Man Hill, Lady Hill and then Lion Riding Carp Hill and Dragon Head Hill, named apparently for their resemblance to lions and dragons. I had difficulty deciphering these and would suggest they used a bit of poetic licence in the nomenclature.

We tried to find Rose's father, who was out working the land, but we failed to locate him amongst the rice paddies, orchards and fields of flourishing crops. Riding on, we continued enjoying the exercise, the warm sun on our backs, as the weather had improved, and, of course, the rich and varied landscape.

The ride was quite challenging in parts with some steep uphill sections, but I had an excellent bike to help me out. We weaved away from the river and then circled back to pedal alongside the Li. Taking a quick break, we watched the fisherfolk at work and boats chugging up and down the broad shimmering watercourse.

On an inland loop, we came across a ramshackle little village with its shop-cum-bar, which was the centre of the community. We stopped for a drink and a snack, and they immediately invited me to play pool with some youngsters. The children were still off school for the New Year holidays.

It ended up with me playing the local champ in front of the largest gallery I had ever performed. The young man boldly wagered 5 RMB (50p), and I felt obliged to accept the challenge. Not playing to my optimum (which requires a few beers), I lost on the black, which seemed an acceptable and diplomatic result.

Groups of old men were drinking and playing various card games, dominoes or mah-jong. Games were conducted with typical enthusiasm, shouts, laughter, and the slamming down of tiles or cards. It was an excellent insight into simple rural life in China. They seemed a friendly and happy bunch.

We bade our new friends goodbye, with some children running alongside us, shouting in glee until they ran out of steam at the edge of the village. Heading back to the riverside, the two others, Ralph and Simon, who had ridden and chatted together for the entire trip, decided they would take a boat back into town. Rose and I continued on our planned journey.

Having ridden another 20km or so on a long circuit before getting back to Yangzhou. I certainly knew that I had had a decent ride.

I met up with Rose later for a drink, and we talked about going for a long hike that she thought I would appreciate the next day.

The following morning, a volley of loud explosions awoke me. I jumped out of bed and looked out of the window to see what was happening. The racket was coming from hundreds of firecrackers - red rolls of crackers like oversized caps for toy guns. Youngsters lay them out on the pavement and set them alight. The resultant detonations reverberated around the buildings and the nearby limestone stacks. The barrage continued for at least half an hour and was phenomenally loud. It was the customary celebration for the end of Chinese New Year's festivities.

I met up with Rose a little while later, as planned, but she appeared to be distinctly unenthused about the prospects of a long hike. It seemed she had failed to drum up any more takers or had something more lucrative on offer. She asked me to pay more than double the rate agreed upon the previous evening, and I declined.

The weather was not so great anyway, being dull, grey and drizzly, with many of the surrounding hills hidden from view. We parted company amicably enough, and I ordered some breakfast in the café where we were sitting on Foreigner St.

I pondered my situation. I could go for a walk by myself but ruled that out because of the weather and not knowing where to go. Toying with my second coffee, I decided I would move on.

Chapter 8
GUILIN

I picked up my bag from the hotel around the corner and headed down to the riverside, where I had previously seen minibuses bound for Guilin milling around. That would be my next port of call.

I was not in any great hurry, Guilin being only an hour away, and regular small local buses were coming and going all the time by the look of things.

A boatload of pomelos had just come into the quayside, and dozens of prospective purchasers had gathered around. They intended to sell them on and were filling panniers, bicycle carts and hand barrows while bargaining with the wholesaler. Having completed her deal, one woman tottered off down the road with huge piles of fruit in two baskets balanced on a yoke. I did not envy her.

As well as being a popular destination for foreign visitors (particularly in the peak season), Yangzhou was becoming increasingly fashionable with growing numbers of domestic tourists. Domestic tourism was booming because of China's thriving economy. There was now a growing number of relatively prosperous Chinese keen to travel beyond their immediate home regions.

Being used to being told what to do in their normal day-to-day life, groups of these tourists, all in matching coloured baseball caps, followed their guide. The guide held up a pole with a matching flag at the top, down the street. These lengthy crocodiles walked past me on their way further along the quay to take boat trips down the River Li.

It was fascinating taking in all the river port activity. Further down, a group of men and women were loading an open boat with long spars of softwood. The timbers were about twelve feet long, of differing diameters, though, which looked to be mainly around 9 inches. The boss kept putting a gauge across to check precisely the volume of wood being loaded and shouting the results to a young girl to record. It was going to be a long, hard job to fill the hold.

It was now close to 11 am, and I felt I should head off. Getting a minibus was straightforward, and I was soon in a half-full vehicle, taking over the front seat for the best view.

The driver negotiated the haphazardly parked vehicles at the riverside before we reached the empty road to Guilin as the weather closed in and it started drizzling. I concluded that travelling onward rather than going for a lengthy hike in the rain was the right option.

Cloud and mist shrouded the tops of the spectacular karst outcrops, and pomelo sellers sat at the roadside on their haunches looking quite miserable beside their little yellow pyramids. They were only protected by flimsy plastic ponchos as the rain came down even harder.

After about an hour, we arrived in Guilin, which looked less than inspiring in the grey and the damp. As the bus dropped me in the centre of town somewhere, my stomach was rumbling. It seemed a long time since breakfast, and my first inclination was to get some lunch. I selected a busy-looking local restaurant. The friendly and enthusiastic staff and several customers helped me to make my meal choice. They seemed surprised at having a Westerner in their midst, and despite the language barrier, we all enjoyed interacting and had quite a laugh. I ended up with a tasty and healthy meal of fried vegetables and lean pork.

Soon, having satisfied my hunger, I would have to find some accommodation. But first, I wanted to locate the station. I had decided I should look into taking a train as I was proposing to go a long way west and south, to Kunming and beyond. I felt a train would be a more comfortable option than a coach for a lengthier trip.

The station was not far, and I made a mental note of where exactly it was, then continued searching for somewhere to stay. In my experience, there usually are plenty of options around a train station, but it did not look that promising here.

After walking around some scruffy back streets for twenty minutes, though, I found somewhere. It was an unprepossessing place in an austere concrete block, but I negotiated the rate down from 130 RMB to 60 RMB, which was a satisfactory result. The staff were rather offhand and miserable, but the room was spacious and acceptable, so I offloaded my rucksack and headed back out to the station.

I knew this would not be straightforward. One member of staff said there was no train to Kunming for five days. Another gave me a price of 460 RMB for the next day, which seemed expensive according to what I had discerned from a notice board. However, I had seen a 'Foreigner' window which would open in ten minutes, so I waited.

There was no queue, so as soon as the little window opened, I could secure a ticket for the next day's afternoon departure to Kunming at the advertised rate of 268 RMB. This was for what they termed a 'hard sleeper'. Excellent. Accommodation and onward travel arrangements sorted, I set off to check out the city a little more in a positive frame of mind.

Guilin is a large city with a population approaching five million people. The city's key industries were processing local agricultural produce, electronics, pharmaceuticals and rubber. It was also big in condoms.

However, with its location on the picturesque Li River and set in the middle of the fascinating and beautiful karst scenery the region is renowned for, it was also a popular tourist destination. Not least with the relatively new, burgeoning Chinese tourist market.

I strolled the length of Zhongshan Zhong Hu, a wide boulevard, home to many upmarket hotels, retail emporia, and restaurants. There were also many more substantial buildings under construction along both sides. Indeed, the city appeared to be undergoing a considerable renaissance costing quite a few million or even a billion yen.

They had paved the broad pedestrianised areas in marble, which looked terrific but offered minimal traction in the wet. As I could confirm when I nearly came a cropper, almost slipping over at one point.

I cut down a little side street, though, and found that Zhongshan Zhong was very much a façade and behind the gleaming new buildings were drab grey concrete apartment blocks. It was an area of unpaved, muddy, potholed and rubbish-strewn streets and many signs of underlying poverty.

A large ornamental lake, Shan Hu, with extensive landscaping and parkland surrounding its sparkling waters (as the sun put in a brief appearance), formed an impressive centrepiece of the city. Two large pagodas were under construction in the middle. Close by was the new Central Square, an extensive pedestrian-only piazza where McDonald's golden arches took pride of place.

Many trendy businesses, coffee shops and speciality restaurants catering to the tourist trade had sprung up in this part of town. Outside one restaurant, a chef in his immaculate whites was attending to a barbeque, focussing on his pièce de résistance, a barbequed terrier complete with teeth and tail rotating on a spit above the hot coals.

The weather turned drizzly again, and it was getting cold such that my breath was condensing. I decided I would head back, have a warming shower, and put on some clean, dry clothes.

The two receptionists at my hotel barely looked up from their knitting as I crossed the foyer. When I reached level two, I got the same lack of response from the floor attendant stationed at her desk.

There were no towels or coffee in my room, but there was a kettle. I politely asked the floor attendant for both and got a grunt in return. Someone brought some hot water for my coffee a little while later, but no towel.

After asking again, I finally got a towel and was ready for the much anticipated shower.

There was no hot water.

At all.

Great.

With a towel around my waist, I marched off down the corridor. I explained my predicament to the grumpy lady.

"No."

"No."

"No hot water," was all I got from her.

I remonstrated and acted out my requirements to emphasise I wanted a shower. The less-than-enthusiastic employee dragged herself away from her knitting to bring me two buckets of boiling water from the bowels of the building.

I had to make do the best I could and be grateful for small mercies.

The room itself was fine, if a little grubby, with a few bits of shabby paintwork and broken or missing handles, but it was okay. Spacious, with a comfortable double bed, were the plus points, but service was definitely not all it could have been. And it would have been nice to have had a working shower and hot water.

Having sluiced myself down as best I could and put some fresh clothes on, I felt ready to launch myself on Guilin for the evening. I was now dressed warmly as it was a chilly night, and thankfully it was no longer raining.

The city was quite vivacious. Thousands of people were out and about on the streets. Firecrackers were going off, and street entertainers were acting out little playlets and operettas, singers, guitarists, accordion players and other random musicians entertained their own little pockets of supporters. Two guys and a young woman playing some soulful and plaintive music on the Chinese violin, the two-stringed erhus. They performed well, and I threw a few coins into the hat in appreciation.

Food hawkers were doing a roaring trade, and there was a sickly all-pervading, the almost edible aroma in the air from the oriental equivalent of toffee apples, doughnuts and candy floss stalls.

A fantastic array of flashing multicoloured neon lights and regular bursts of fireworks illuminated the sky. Loudspeakers on lamp posts screeched out Chinese pop or folk tunes. I now actually understood that Chinese New Year celebrations last an entire month.

Groups of Chinese tourists with their coloured baseball caps were being herded through the melee by their team leaders. From what I saw, I was the only Westerner on parade.

Cute little toddlers seemed delighted with their helium balloons and cheap cuddly toys, although one little boy was crying his eyes out. He was watching distraught, as his precious balloon rose rapidly into the night sky to be lost forever.

On and around park benches, clusters of old men played various games involving noisy audience participation, shouting, clapping, and high-fiving. Bundles of money changed hands regularly.

In the main square, an excellent male vocalist received an appreciative reception for his efforts from the sizeable crowd. Over the road, a succession of elaborate floats drew regular oohs and ah's from the family audience. With the cold and misty night air, the atmosphere was like an old-fashioned bonfire night back home.

I now felt it was time to eat. It was a little tricky to discern amongst the sea of flashing neon signage, all in Chinese lettering, what exactly was a restaurant and what was a shop, beautician, hairdresser or whatever. I happened across one with an English translation, and once I had established that it was, in fact, a restaurant and not a sexual advice centre, I ventured into Come Together.

A calm oasis, reasonably busy but not overly so, this upmarket place suited my requirements exactly for a relaxed evening meal and time to catch up with my book.

The next day on getting up, I, of course, wanted to have a shower and a shave. I tottered off down the corridor to where the harridan was, as usual, knitting away abstractedly. Asking for water just made her angry.

"What! Another bloody shower you had one only yesterday, you despicable cretin," was the gist of her response, roughly translated.

She followed this up with:

"No hot water!"

Another warder, as I now termed them, arrived, basically to back up the first one:

"No hot water!"

"I have gathered that, you miserable old bat. Please get me a couple of buckets like last night."

I was not backing down, and reluctantly they went off to get me some hot water.

"Well, I never! Two showers in two days. Who does he think he is?" I think they said to each other on the way to the stairs.

The train was not due to depart until the afternoon, so I needed somewhere to leave my bag for the day. The left luggage office I had noticed at the station might be the best option. Rather than prevail on the hotel to safeguard my belongings for a few hours. That would have undoubtedly involved more drama, something I did not need.

After my wash down and shave, I packed my stuff and presented myself at the hotel reception. I had paid a deposit on top of the room charge when I checked in. I now had to hang around to see whether they would return this. They dispatched a staff member to give my room the once over. Presumably, she needed to check that I had not nicked a loo roll or a pillow or even the pair of manky flip-flops I had spied in the corner of the room.

The receptionist gave the nod that all was in order and returned my deposit. I could leave after my experience of the Chinese hospitality industry at its very best.

Guilin was wearing its heavy grey overcoat again. I had hoped to go out into the countryside to see some of the karst peaks close up, but it did not seem an option at the moment. In the murky, almost freezing fog conditions, they were barely discernible.

I left my bag in the left luggage room at the station and wandered down to the riverside. By now, the sun was attempting to penetrate the murk, and it was getting a little warmer.

The streets were busy with trucks, buses and thousands of bicycles as everyone went about their business. I considered hiring a bike myself, rusted steel machines with no gears and inadequate brakes I had seen put me off that idea. It didn't seem worth it.

In a country of probably half a billion bicycles, I wondered how many were in anything like tiptop condition. It would not be many. I realised I had been fortunate in Yangzhou to get hold of a brand new mountain bike from the hire shop.

I had seen in Vietnam and Cambodia that small 125cc motorcycles were the most popular form of personal transportation, with a relatively small percentage of bicycles. Hanoi and Ho Chi Min City had been awash with motorbikes. In China, the situation was reversed.

Down by the broad Li River, I walked along the wide marble promenade. Even in the gloom, the eye-catching rock formations were impressive. I could make out 'Elephant's Trunk', 'Wave Subduing Hill' and 'Tunnel Hill'.

Ranks of tourist boats were moored up along the river jetties, awaiting the spring and summer seasons, when they would be endlessly busy. A few houseboats with two or three bamboo rafts floating astern with dark, brooding cormorants sitting on decks, preening themselves, were also tied up. The fishing community here was like the one I had seen in Yangzhou. They did not seem interested in fishing on this drab, cold day, and I couldn't blame them.

At the end of the promenade, I found the entrance to Elephant Trunk Park and paid my 20 RMB admission fee. The park was quite a treat. They had pleasantly laid it out with stone walkways and bridges over watercourses diverted from the river, neatly cropped lawns and extensive and colourful flowerbeds.

The soaring rocky outcrop, which gave the park its name, did indeed look like an elephant putting its trunk into the water for a drink, overlooked the complete area.

It pleased me to make the connection readily enough with the elephant. Other monoliths such as 'Grandpa watching an apple', 'Frog crossing the river' and 'Miller at work' were considerably more difficult, that is to say impossible, to interpret.

I climbed the two hundred steps to the top of Elephant Hill. Unfortunately, the visibility was not the best to enjoy the ordinarily extensive and panoramic views, but it was good to have done the ascent all the same. It was still quite breathtaking to be so high above the wide meandering river and see the dozens of fantastic examples of unique limestone karst scenery spread out before me.

It was now time for me to make my way back to the station and leave Guilin.

About twenty minutes before departure, they corralled all the passengers into the number 1 waiting room at the station. I just went along with the flow.

Once an official had checked all the tickets and said something I did not understand, there was a mad stampede for the train. Philosophically, I took my time as I felt I had my ticket with the designated seat/bed number printed on it, so I should be okay without having to rush.

That was the case, and I soon found the carriage and my allotted middle-tier berth with no problem. The berth was effectively a sizeable single bed with a decent mattress that stayed down for the entire journey. It was far better than my expectations.

I also quickly realised that my middle bunk was the best bet. The bottom one was it seemed used by all and sundry as a seat during the day. While the top bed was too high and too close to the ceiling to have any view out of the window.

There were additional pull-down seats opposite the lowest beds for daytime use. It was a most satisfactory arrangement and far superior to the cramped hard seat I had had to endure on a long overnight trip in Australia some months earlier.

With my rucksack stored in the commodious luggage area, I set out my stall, organising myself on my bunk. I positioned myself to have a good view out of the window and settled down with my book and Walkman to enjoy a relaxing journey - all thirty hours of it.

This journey would be my longest-ever single leg of travel, overtaking my Perth to Broome coach journey of a few months previously. It would also knock a long boat delivery trip I once undertook from Ipswich to Chichester into second place. Those were mere twenty-seven-hour stretches.

An hour into the journey, we passed through a widespread area of stunning, tightly arranged terraces, which looked distinctly eerie in the murky mist. This spectacular landscape, I quickly realised, was the centuries-old man-made Longxi rice terraces of Longsheng. The Yao minority hill tribe people had farmed this incredible environment for centuries with their agricultural constructions stretching up to the top of a range of 500m lofty peaks.

I quickly checked my *Lonely Planet* to confirm my thoughts whilst feasting my eyes on the wonderful hand crafted terraces.

Once through the Longsheng area and realising I had not eaten since a light breakfast, I decided it was time to venture down to the restaurant car. All the locals in my carriage had also decided it was mealtime. They, however, would give the restaurant a miss, gathering instead around a large stainless steel samovar at the end of the carriage. They existed solely on noodles or rice and adding boiling water for a basic speedy meal.

The restaurant car was virtually empty, with the locals all self-catering. I had to resort to the small language section in my *Lonely Planet* to order some food, but that was straightforward. The most hospitable server seemed to find it fun helping to decipher my requirements.

Enjoying my chicken, fried rice, and a wide range of spicy vegetables, the dark outside world slipped by. The meal was washed down with a couple of bottles of palatable beer. It was a highly satisfying experience. I stayed in my restaurant seat for a while, reading and writing, as it was pleasantly quiet. Later I returned to my bunk and crashed out - the rhythmic sounds of the wheels on the tracks and the motion of the carriages were satisfyingly soporific.

Upon waking, I took my time, waiting for the rush to die down. After things became quieter, I made use of the excellent and clean facilities for my ablutions before heading to the restaurant car for breakfast. This train travel lark was proving most enjoyable.

Again, I stayed in the restaurant car for a while after I had eaten. Enjoying several coffees, I contemplated the ever-changing vista as we charged west and south towards Kunming.

A little later, they held a staff meeting. There was a sizeable gathering of employees in khaki military-style uniforms with peaked caps, fancy epaulettes, and lots of gold brocade. It was reminiscent of the start of *Hill Street Blues. Let's be careful out there.* They all sat down to listen attentively to what their boss had to say. There were no other customers in the restaurant car.

The other passengers all seemed happy to make their tea and rice or noodles from the samovars and use the day seats and the lowest beds to sit and chat and play card games.

I spent most of the morning in the restaurant carriage. Once the staff meeting had finished, I was on my own and watched the spectacular mountainous scenery flashing by. We climbed ever onward towards Kunming, which lies at a height of nearly 2000m.

Innumerable tunnels had been built to help navigate the inhospitable terrain; the line's construction was unquestionably a significant feat of engineering. The railway had played a critical role in opening up access to the once-remote southwest of the country.

By the time I returned to the buffet car for a late lunch after an hour of relaxing and reading on my bunk, the sky had become a deep cloudless blue. This was most welcome after a few days of cloudy, grey gloom.

We were now crossing a high plateau with dramatic pine-clad mountain views in the distance. Intricately terraced hillsides laid out before me like a giant jigsaw puzzle. Predominantly, the picture was of browns and various shades of green and slashed by silvery streams in the foreground. There were just a few tiny hamlets of ramshackle wood and thatch construction as evidence of any habitation.

An hour further on (about twenty-five hours into the journey), there was little sign of cultivation. The altitude was probably too high, and they had left the region to nature with soaring snow-capped peaks, bare rock scree, coarse grass and scrawny pines. It was a truly majestic, rugged landscape. We were now diving into tunnels regularly, this being the only way trains could overcome the mountainous terrain.

After thirty and a half hours, we rolled into Kunming pretty much on time.

Chapter 9

KUNMING AND DALI

Early the following day, I awoke to incredible blue skies and warming sunshine, which lifted my spirits immediately. I had found some accommodation readily enough the previous evening at the Camellia hotel. This pleasant enough place had standard rooms and some quality provision for backpackers as shared bedrooms for three or four. I secured a bed in a large triple room for a mere 25 RMB a night.

When I stepped out to see what Kunming offered, my exploration attire was shorts and sandals. After a few days of shivering temperatures and gloomy drizzle, this was a significant and welcome change.

Before I ventured out, I could apply for a visa to Laos. They had conveniently found a home for the consulate within the hotel. I was planning to travel to that country after leaving SW China.

My revised plan was now to stay a few days in Kunming, a city of three-and-a-half-million people, until I could pick my visa up. I would then take a sleeper train on to Dali.

I walked for several miles, enjoying the warmth and ambience. The city, at first sight, appeared a little uninspiring. However, I could unearth some hidden traditional areas amongst the overwhelming amount of substantial construction work going on. Thousands of tons of glass and steel were replacing vast swathes of wonderful old wooden shophouses in the name of progress.

As I walked, I came across a hairdressing establishment. A happy couple in all their wedding finery who were having a 'his and hers' hairdo before the ceremony. Bizarrely (I thought) the bride-to-be had to wait patiently whilst the hairdresser finished her groom's blow-dry.

On one of the principal thoroughfares, Jimbi Lu, I marvelled at the displays of colourful cherry blossoms and the deep red camellias. I also passed several florists, whose ornate floral presentations were fantastic. They must have taken hours of skilful patience to achieve. The sheer scale, range of colours and overall magnificence of the blooms on display in the florists in Kunming were a significant highlight of the city for me.

I later came across a large flower market, which was an absolute riot of colour, and reinforced the idea of Kunming being known as the city of flowers. Or indeed, as I read in some marketing blurb, 'The City of Eternal Spring'. There were lots of ladies sitting fabricating highly ornate and colourful bouquets for sale or order.

The city also boasted several large and beautiful green open spaces. I found Cuihu Park skirting Green Lake to be a most pleasant place to wander in the Spring sunshine. Many locals were out enjoying a walk, playing with their toddlers, flying kites or feeding the birds. Older chaps played mah jong with their friends on park benches.

I had a coffee and a snack at a charming and quite genteel little teahouse close to the park. This was run by an elegant lady with a tall beehive hairdo looking like a refugee from a sixties American girl vocal group. I would not normally have eaten, but she was very persuasive in encouraging me to try some of her homemade pastries.

After my highly civilised break, I walked up to the northern edge of the park. I had picked up this as being the livelier, more bohemian and student-orientated part of town.

At a French-themed bar which had drawn me in, an inquisitive young student sat sipping a coffee surrounded by books and files. Vivienne, as she said her name was, asked if I was happy to chat as she enjoyed talking with native English speakers.

"I am studying here in Beijing, but my family now live in California," she told me.

She was seventeen and in her final school year, but currently on holiday from school.

"School is hard work, but I want to do well so that I can be a television journalist."

"What are your school hours like?" I asked, knowing them to be more rigorous than back home.

"We are at school from 7.30 in the morning until 5.30 pm Monday to Friday, and we do four hours on Saturday and Sunday mornings, so it is quite hard. My friend is at school in England, and she says the hours are easy there."

She asked me about the royal family (not my specialist subject) and told me she had been a massive fan of Princess Diana.

"President Bush does not speak very good English," she later offered.

I vaguely remember seeing a news clip of a tongue-tied President being asked some tricky questions by a group of Chinese students. He did not look at all comfortable.

It was most engaging to chat with such a bright girl who I was sure would follow her dreams and become a broadcaster. She will be on CNN soon enough.

Walking back down to Juibi Lu and along for a short while, I crossed to Dongsi Joe, where I could see some interesting wooden buildings. This was another area that had avoided the wrecking balls for the moment. Many of the old wooden shophouses were decorated with ornate carvings and gold and scarlet-painted dragons. They had largely been transformed into trendy bars and restaurants.

It was about time for a beer by now, and I selected an exceptionally attractively restored and refurbished place for a sundowner. One of the dozen staff hanging around - it was quiet - brought me a drink over as I got my *Lonely Planet* guide and notebook out and started writing.

Head down, concentrating, I could feel people close by. I looked up to see about eight uniformed staff members standing within a few inches of me staring at what I was doing. They considered me quite an interesting and rare specimen. After finishing my drink and still surrounded by this corps of inquisitive Chinese, I moved off as I had had enough of them gawping at me.

A couple of bars along, I was pleased to find something more to my liking. The place was more of an ex-pat bar with a decent rocky soundtrack playing and some other travellers with whom to chat. I met a couple of Aussies, a Canadian and a Dutch guy (who was also staying at the Camellia). The evening progressed after we became acquainted over a few beers.

Moving on to another cool bar in another beautiful old restored wooden building run by a friendly Burmese chap, we settled down for some more beers. We then played drinking games with a group of local lads in their early twenties, celebrating a school reunion. It surprised me to find, amongst their repertoire of fun contests, games with which I was familiar; they applied drinking forfeits to the classic scissors, paper, stone game. I could also teach them the standard rugby club drinking game of spoof.

These young Chinese students all spoke passable English, and we enjoyed an alcohol-induced cultural exchange for a couple of hours or more.

The next morning, after a pretty awful buffet breakfast I hadn't realised was part of my package but probably would have been happy to have remained ignorant of, I continued my explorations of Kunming. I came across a fascinating street market with displays of antiques, pottery, antiquarian books and ancient bric-a-bac on sale. There was also a stall selling wonderful bonsai trees that I enjoyed studying in close detail. Making a meticulous examination of these tiny, beautiful, mature plants in miniature completely captivated me.

In the balmy spring weather under the cherry and magnolia blossom, there were family groups out strolling. Or else sitting chatting at one of the many pavement cafes. The soft warm air was full of birdsong, and I was finding Kunming all quite enchanting.

Three or four prospective young shoe shiners quickly surrounded me as I grabbed a coffee to remove the taste of the disgusting breakfast. After shooing them off, I sat and read for a while at the pavement table.

I reflected I would probably spend a little longer in this pleasant enough city with the delay in obtaining my visa, but I was pretty optimistic about the situation. It was not a terrible place to be.

Close to the city centre, I later came across a row of charming traditional Muslim restaurants. These were incongruously set in amongst modern Kunming's predominant and overwhelming glass and steel towers. I pondered this and realised that the region had the highest proportion of ethnic minorities in the whole of China. Several of these minority groups, such as the Hui, are Muslims, hence the rows of halal food outlets.

Although the dominant and ubiquitous Han made up 80% of the population of the Yunnan province, of which Kunming is the capital city, a dozen or more ethnic minority groups make up the other fifth. The Yi, originally from Burma and Thailand, is the most extensive grouping.

I appreciated this ethnic and cultural mix. It made the region far more culturally, historically, and linguistically diverse. There was a more interesting mix of different cuisines, modes of dress, and customs in evidence. It was certainly not as homogeneous as the more easterly regions of this vast country.

I had a snack to keep me going and headed for my new local, the Burmese guy's place, in the early evening. More ex-pats were about on this Saturday evening, having an early drink in anticipation of England's Six Nations match against the French. I quickly became involved with a group that included four or five French chaps, three Englishmen, two Scandinavians, a Canadian, and an Aussie with a Chinese girlfriend.

We had a good laugh and a few rounds of beers before the game, but once the match was underway, I was not so upbeat. After a superb performance last time out, the England team were under the cosh in the first half. The French enjoyed a brilliant opening twenty minutes and rattled along to a 17-0 lead. With two tries from fly half Merceron and one from the classy number eight Harinordorquy the French were well in control. The French pack was proving too strong for us. England fought back but could never fully claw the situation back from those early reverses and went down 20-15, putting an immediate end to any Grand Slam dreams.

The next morning, after a bit of a lie-in and, for obvious reasons, skipping the awful buffet, I ventured out in the continuing warming sunshine to discover a little more of the city.

Not far into my walk, I met a young man handing out leaflets for English conversation classes. He had recognised me as someone who potentially spoke English and who might help him. He told me he would appreciate it if I could go along for an hour to chat with Chinese nationals who were keen to learn conversational English. Feeling a little generous-spirited, I agreed.

I went along to a small hall where I chatted with a group of a dozen young Chinese students. A couple of other Chinese English speakers were there, but the students wanted some interaction with the real McCoy.

I stayed for about an hour; the scholars were very enthusiastic and prepared to get the pronunciation correct and pick up more vocabulary, but I found it quite intensive. Session over, my recruiter thanked me and felt I had done my good deed for the day.

Later, I went back to pick up my visa before going to the station to book my ticket for the overnight sleeper for Dali. The latter was once an important staging post on the infamous Burma Road.

While handing my rucksack in for storage, I stupidly put my small day bag down on the floor (it just had a book, notebook, map, sunscreen, and Walkman in it). Seconds later, out of the corner of my eye, I saw a young man snatch it up and sprint off. I chased him over the concourse and out into the road. I was gaining on the thief as we weaved in and out of surprised pedestrians. He just dropped my bag, and I decided that discretion was the better part of valour and aborted the chase to just rescue my belongings.

Having averted a mini-drama, I could now enjoy my last afternoon and evening in Kunming before heading back for the station and taking the 10.35 pm train.

Many families were out again in the parks as it was such a lovely sunny Sunday afternoon. However, it was not a day of rest for the many construction workers. These guys were hard at it on the scores of significant construction and civil engineering projects underway throughout the city centre. They were working on rapidly launching Kunming headlong into the 21st century.

I walked past a hospital and spotted a young doctor, stethoscope still around his neck, leaning against an outside wall having a cigarette break. I thought it was hardly an excellent advert for the profession. However, many Chinese, including physicians, still saw smoking as a harmless pleasure and not the killer we acknowledge it to be in the West.

Cutting through a shopping mall by way of a shortcut it amazed me to see the sheer volume of mobile phones for sale in one place. There was a vast army of junior assistants demonstrating and selling the latest models to enthusiastic would-be purchasers. China was undergoing a significant revolution in personal telephone devices. This confirmed what I had heard some months back when in Malacca.

I spent most of the evening relaxing over a meal, a couple of drinks and a bit of reading before going to catch my train. The overnight train would reach Dali at some ungodly hour in the morning, 5 am or so. As it was only a journey of around 350km, it was not an express trip by any stretch of the imagination.

I did not sleep as well as I had on the train that brought me to Kunming. My berth was at the end of the carriage, and passengers slammed the door regularly throughout the night as they embarked or disembarked. This meant getting any decent shuteye was difficult. Emerging after just a few hours of broken sleep into the cold and dark, drizzly pre-dawn was not ideal. I was at Xiaguan, as Dali City is alternatively known, not feeling at my most optimistic, and definitely needing more sleep. Being hemmed in by a swarm of yelling and aggressively gesticulating touts marketing their guesthouses, bus tours or taxi rides did not improve my state of mind.

I had a map, but it only marked the station at the extreme western edge with an arrow showing 'station 2km'.

Dismissing the rabble from my presence with an imperious sweep of my arm, I marched off, hoping that I had deciphered my orientation correctly. Amongst the shouts from the mob, I had heard an offer of 50 RMB for a taxi to Dali town, which lay some 12km or so away. My guidebook had suggested the bus fare was just over one RMB. Profiteering bastards, I thought miserably.

After half an hour - as the sky was lightening and the city was waking up to face the day - I could confirm I was walking in the right direction. Noodle shops seemed to do a roaring trade, with workers grabbing a quick breakfast.

I found the bus station, could pay the measly one-and-a-half RMB fare, and was soon on my way to old town Dali.

Skirting the ear-shaped Lake Erhai, which lay to my right, from our current elevation of around 2000m, I could see the snow-tipped peaks of the Cangshan range to the west. This epic range rose upwards to heights of 4000m plus. The mountains looked bleak and treeless, and there was much evidence of quarrying along the route. Great scars carved into the landscape. There was a rainbow of different colours, showing the wide range of different metamorphic stone being extracted from the country rock above us on the steep flanks.

Several magnificent waterfalls cascaded down from up high.

Rock crushing, the production of different-sized aggregates, monumental masonry and the dressing of huge beautifully coloured marble blocks was the primary industry in the area. This place was rock central.

Bai people, a Tibeto-Burmese ethnic grouping, dominated the area. Many traditionally dressed women were out in force selling handmade products, embroidery and suchlike. They were operating from makeshift stalls on the roadside along the ribbon of small villages we passed through.

Bai means white in Chinese and refers to the people's use of a copious amount of white in their traditional dress. They also wore a lot of silver jewellery, embroidered white shoes and coloured sleeveless jackets.

While the Bai were proud of their heritage, they were generally happy enough to be absorbed into the mainstream Chinese (Han) way of life. However, they remained pragmatic about using their ethnic minority status. They understood that wearing their traditional dress and selling their handcrafted wares, and acting as guides for Han tourists, could prove quite lucrative.

The bus came to a halt in Dali right outside Jim's Tibetan Guesthouse, where I had earmarked to stay. So, believing this to be serendipitous, I grabbed my bag and hopped off. A decent enough room with a large double bed and squishy feather mattress soon became my temporary home.

For once, the bed seemed more attractive than the option of going out to explore. I was exhausted, so I decided a couple of hours of sleep were in order.

After my doze, I showered and changed and ventured out into town. The setting for the small ancient city was most striking. Sat on the edge of Lake Erhai with magnificent peaks rising inexorably behind the settlement to the west, it was an idyllic place. It was understandably popular with western backpackers and Chinese tourists alike. The ageless narrow cobbled streets and houses constructed of stone and wood were wonderfully evocative of long-gone days.

However, there was evidence that the authorities had gentrified the old city somewhat. Ancient tumbling city walls and gates were being rebuilt to create a new 'Old Dali.' This Disneyfication was being undertaken to attract the burgeoning Chinese middle classes. The latter were embracing tourism to this area in their droves.

I was a little disappointed with this treatment of the place.

In the middle of town, I quickly found Huguo Lu or Foreigner Street. This was a large pedestrianised area crammed with shops, cafes, restaurants, guesthouses, souvenir places, and many market stalls. The latter were manned by Bai women in all their traditional finery selling their craftwork. Carved marble products and ethnic clothing outlets were also much in evidence.

At the bottom of Huguo Lu was Fuxing Lu, which appeared to be stacked with souvenir shops catering solely for the home tourism market. Groups of tourists, wearing the, by now, familiar identical coloured baseball caps, were walking in a crocodile formation behind a flag-bearing Bai woman in her full traditional regalia. Comically, they looked to the right or left in unison as instructed by their guide as she pointed out particular features or buildings.

The touristy centre was not really for me, so I escaped finding some back streets of old wooden buildings with distinctive orange roof tiling. Many buildings had guttering, sporting impressive amounts of grass and weeds and even small trees sprouting out from them.

I came across a local's market. Here, I saw hundreds of chickens, geese, and ducks, as well as thousands of their very young offspring chirping away incessantly, imprisoned in stacks of woven reed baskets. A group of women were sitting on small stools in front of a row of wet and bloody concrete-floored, open-fronted slaughterhouses. They were chatting away constantly and nonchalantly. An unsuspecting chicken would be grabbed every few seconds and swiftly have its throat cut. It would then be tossed, still squawking, into a forty-gallon drum alongside. Barely looking at the poor birds, they were skilfully dispatching them with indecent haste.

Further down the market, in the fresh vegetable section, vast bunches of produce were being placed into large traditional woven baskets. Or else modern garishly coloured plastic ones. They strapped goods onto the backs of the purchasers who then wandered off homewards.

It was now around 4 pm, so the market was just about closing up. The weather had taken a turn for the worse - low cloud had descended, and it was drizzling heavily. Dali was at a low latitude, almost in the tropics. However, its elevation of nearly 2000m affected temperatures considerably, and it now felt scarcely above freezing.

Impulsively, as the cold got to me, I looked around for somewhere I could buy a top. I felt I needed another layer to keep the cold at bay. I found some very nice locally made, quite heavy-duty 100% hemp tops (they grew hemp extensively throughout the area) but could find nothing of my size. The shop owner said he could knock me one up within the hour, which I thought was great.

After he had taken details of my vital statistics, I retreated to a relatively warm little café. Here, I could await the delivery of my made-to-measure, hand-tailored garment. I say relatively warm as the only heat source was a little pot of glowing charcoal which was fighting a losing battle against the elements.

My tailor later delivered my new item of clothing, which fitted a treat, and I paid the man a modest amount of RMB. However, even with the additional layer on, as night fell and the temperatures plummeted further, keeping warm became a challenge all evening.

I stopped for something to eat at another little cafe, which was okay, but I was still cold. Using the little charcoal burners was not very effective.

Back at Jim's, his front room, which doubled as a bar, was toasty warm. There was a far more substantial charcoal fire in the corner, blasting heat out like a furnace, which was much appreciated. A bit of a party was underway, with lots of empty bottles on the tables and a most convivial atmosphere building.

Before I knew it, they had made the introductions, and I had a drink in my hand. Someone had swiftly handed me a large glass of Jim's speciality cocktail. This was a potent mix of local corn wine plus herbs, spices and roots, including ginseng and ginger and other exotic additions. It tasted pretty good. We were a motley group of travellers and a collection of locals in the far corner of the bar, all intent on enjoying a few drinks and having a chat.

After a few rounds of drinks, some local snacks and some lively chat, we called it a day around midnight. I was happy to dive under my duvet, having done my bit for anglo-sino relations.

I had planned to explore the lakeside and the surrounding area by bike the next day, but the weather was not good. With virtually freezing fog conditions, I quickly changed my plans and decided to move on.

Chapter 10

A BAI HOMESTAY IN MY SHANGRI LA

I had picked up a postcard in one of Dali's little cafes and decided I would not go straight to Lijiang but visit what they called a 'Bai homestay'. The card advertised the local equivalent of bed-and-breakfast accommodation. Visitors would be put up with a traditional Bai family in a small village called Shaxi, roughly halfway between Dali and Lijiang.

I took a final stroll around some more of Dali's little lanes and found somewhere for breakfast before walking out to the main highway to await a local bus.

They only had the bus destination boards marked up in Chinese. Someone had told me to look for the number 20, but as the buses rarely displayed a number, this was not tremendously helpful.

Eventually the appropriate vehicle spluttered to a halt, and I squeezed myself into a narrow hard seat on the battered old bus. The route I was travelling was some 90km, basically the entire length of Lake Erhai and beyond. So I had to come to terms with a less-than-comfortable trip for a couple of hours.

As I settled into my limited space, I reflected on my visit to Dali.

I decided I was a little ambivalent about the place. While retaining a lot of its old historical charm and atmosphere, much of the town was undergoing a major rebuilding programme. Dali of the past was being re-imagined as a tourist attraction for the Chinese market of the future.

The authorities were also looking to cater for the western backpacking crowd. Internet cafes, banana pancake and pizza outlets, as well as the by-products of the feral hemp plants found throughout the area, were more than acceptable to many of the younger backpackers coming to the area. However, for me, the place's transformation into a tourist mecca had eroded more than a little of the town's authenticity. Dali was in danger of losing its soul.

Initially, the route up to Jianchuan was relatively straightforward. The highway followed the lakeside and was relatively flat and in good condition. Vast, brooding mountains rose through the clouds to our left-hand side. We then reached the end of the lakeside road. The road then narrowed, and the driver swung the ancient spluttering and belching charabanc westwards up an increasingly steep slope. We wound our way up the potholed road to emerge on a plateau some miles further on.

The bus continued along a flattish, straight road across an area of intensively cultivated land before the road narrowed and climbed again. Twisting round a series of hairpin bends, we emerged on to a further tableland surrounded by rugged peaks.

This time, closely spaced trees flanked the road with the bottom foot or two painted white. The painting was presumably to deter animals and insects which might otherwise attack the bark. These reminded me of plane trees skirting the roads in rural France. The painting there being for headlights to identify the edge of the road at night time rather than deterring damage by the local fauna.

As well as pockets of well-cultivated smallholdings, it was apparent that using the mountain's natural resources was the primary industry in the region. Manufacture of lime and cement, making bricks and tiles, crushing rock, and carving intricate stone decorations or memorials was very much in evidence. There were also small factories making breeze blocks and firing wood to make charcoal briquettes. Several villages we passed through were completely white from the lime dust from the many cement manufacturing plants.

Further along the route, we passed by a very impressive and substantial new reservoir with huge white lettering designed to be seen from the air on the side of one of the artificial banks. Then, dropping a little into a wide valley with intricately terraced slopes at the extremities, we finally arrived at Jianchuan.

It was a tiny, remote, one-horse town, but it was not my final destination. I had to go on further to an even smaller settlement. At the bus depot, I deciphered which bus would go on to Shaxi, found one, jumped aboard and was off for another twenty-odd kilometres.

This journey took well over an hour as we climbed up higher, tackling tortuous twisting bends overlooking perilously steep gorges. The ancient vehicle's engine screamed in agony at the workload being expected of it. Meanwhile, the sheer rock walls on one side and precipitous slopes slashed with roaring, surging white water on the other made for a hair-raising trip.

As we approached the village, the bus overflowing with passengers already was required to absorb a crowd of young school children. Their shrill chatter added considerably to the already noisy and smoky atmosphere.

The narrow road became cobbled for the last mile or two, shaking bones and rattling teeth. It also gave the poor abused vehicle's suspension a workout it did not need.

Finally, we all disembarked in the little village of Shaxi. I had a card with the Homestay's address written in both English and Chinese and showed it to a man standing close by. I was looking for Wu Yun Xin of 40, Duan Village, Jianchuan, Yunnan, China, so I was not even staying in Shaxi, but in the hamlet of Duan.

As it transpired, the man, the owner of a nearby shop, and prosperous judging by his appearance, was the homestay owner's uncle and spoke some English. He quickly called his nephew on his mobile phone and then handed the phone to me. The nephew, ironically, was in Dali and apologised for not being there to greet me.

Then he said, "I recognise your voice. Were you in Jim's bar last night?"

He had been with the group of locals in the corner, enjoying Jim's hospitality. Small world. He explained the uncle would drive me to his home and phone his wife to prepare a meal. I thanked him and handed the phone back. A most satisfactory outcome and preferable to wandering around aimlessly in an obscure Chinese hamlet clutching a business card.

So, the friendly chap quickly whisked me out to the delightful Bai settlement of Duan in the shadow of one of the giant mountains out to the west.

With long jet-black hair and an attractive dark oval face, Wu's wife came out to greet me at the end of a path to their house, baby on her hip.

She spoke no English, but we quickly found the right gestures as we walked back to the house. It was quite an extensive property; the main two-storey traditional building faced us over the courtyard, an annexe to the side, to my right, and a utility block with an outdoor kitchen opposite that. There were barns on the fourth side.

She showed me into the annexe, which comprised a large twin-bedded room with a sofa, armchair, and coffee table. Through a door, there was a guest lounge with another couch and chairs, a television and CD system, a small dining area and a fridge stocked with beer. There was also a tray with glasses and a supply of rice wine, a flask of boiling water and a supply of coffee sachets. My hostess went to the CD player and put some music on by a Chinese artist who sounded very much like Enya. It was all looking good.

Using sign language to ask where the ablutions were, my hostess took me outside down the little lane to where I could see the pigsties and the chicken runs. Initially, I thought perhaps she had lost something in the translation. But no, opposite the pigs was a new well-appointed shower and loo constructed of breeze blocks but tiled and smartly finished inside.

Back in my room, I made myself a coffee and sat down to flick through a few English magazines that were on the coffee table. I was told that my meal would arrive shortly.

Ten minutes later, I was tucking into noodle soup, stir-fried vegetables and chicken, rice and two poached eggs. It was perfect.

It was getting considerably colder, though, and as dusk fell, the grandma of the household knocked on my door. She brought in a stand and a small metal bowl filled with hot, glowing charcoals. A heat source inspired me to have another beer, change the CD for a Whitney Houston live concert album and settle down with my book for a while.

The charcoal burned down within the hour, and the combination of the cold and a couple of beers meant I needed to trek out to the pigs. It was pitch black as I negotiated the courtyard and felt for the latch on the gate. I negotiated my way around the styes and huts, located the light switch for the loo and had a pee. And then cautiously found my way back in the pitch-black and eerily silent night.

I decided I did not wish to repeat this process in the middle of the night, and looking around, I saw a couple of wastepaper bins. One was of raffia and would not be fit for purpose, but the other was plastic and would do nicely. I congratulated myself on some sound contingency planning.

Grandma reappeared to freshen up my central heating; I changed Whitney for Madonna, the only other disc available, but luckily another decent live performance CD, and by way of a change cracked open the rice wine. The wine was more like a light spirit in terms of strength, at 20% of alcohol by volume. I added some Pepsi that I had in my rucksack from the bus journey and a few cubes of ice and found it very palatable, as well as being quite soporific.

As I went to bed, I sleepily thought about where I was. I was probably the only westerner in an extremely rural Bai community in Southwest China. In the foothills of the Himalayas, with monstrous peaks towering above me. It was certainly a long way from home.

Waking about 8 am after a good sleep, I trotted across the misty courtyard to say good morning to the animals and undertake my ablutions. Discreetly taking the half-full wastepaper bin with me. On my return, a breakfast of eggs, spicy fried potatoes, mange-tout, rice and toasted goat's cheese was waiting for me. Fresh boiling water was available to make some instant coffee.

I stepped outside after breakfast, sipping my coffee as the welcome sun broke through. However, low clouds still obscured the mountaintops. It felt good to take deep breaths of fresh mountain air.

I made a copy of the rough sketch map of the area pinned to the wall. I had heard from the shopkeeper-uncle the previous day that there would be an enormous market held in town. This, he told me, was quite a major event. So, map in hand, I set off to find where the action was.

When my hostess cleared away my breakfast things, and I got the message across that I was off to market, she smiled approvingly. I, meanwhile, was looking forward to seeing an authentic slice of Chinese rural life.

As I walked down the narrow country lanes, the sun strengthened quickly, and I soon discarded some layers, including my smart new sage green hemp jacket. I felt it was prudent to have enough clothing with me, though, as I had already experienced how the temperature could drop rapidly on these high plateaux.

I was in a broad open valley, a patchwork of bountiful fields of browns, greens and golds stretching to where the mountains rose steeply. With the sky clearing, it was now possible to see to the top of some of these magnificent snow-capped peaks on both sides of the valley.

As I walked down the dusty route, regularly bridging small, fast-moving streams, I could see significant numbers of people joining the main track from smaller side lanes. People were coming down from other small settlements in the area. Many were carrying heavy sacks of pulses or grains on their backs, using a band across their foreheads to spread the load. Others had empty woven panniers intent on filling them at the market.

I became, as usual, a source of much amusement to local kids shouting,

"Hello,"

"Nice to meet you," and

"What is your name?"

Then running away, giggling.

As we drew closer into town, the numbers grew, and a veritable menagerie of creatures heading for market joined us. There were cows, bulls, young weaner calves, water buffalo, donkeys, mules, horses, goats and pigs. All were proceeding contentedly; animals kept in order by an occasional quick tap from a stick as they honked, mooed or bleated their way along.

Just short of town, on the cobbled main road, scores of cyclopses (the ubiquitous single-cylinder diesel engine tractors) and trailers full of produce and people were turning off the highway into Shaxi. There were also scores of overladen minibuses clogging up the route.

The market took over the whole town, and it was apparent that the gathering was a major weekly event.

While most of the people attending the market were Bai with their predominantly white outfits, coloured sleeveless jackets, and embroidered shoes, there were also many Naxi. The latter were wearing their distinctive indigo outfits topped with black turbans. The Yi, with their very colourful and elaborately embroidered attire, were also out in force. Han people were almost conspicuous by their absence.

Roughly halfway between Dali and Lijiang, Shaxi's market was famous throughout the Yunnan region. Its history went back to the fourteenth century when the settlement first came to prominence as a caravan town on the tea and horse-trading route.

I felt privileged to have stumbled on such a historic spot where I was witnessing living history.

I finally reached the centre of town, the 'Sideng', or sizeable market square, which was the focal point of proceedings. Trading activities spread throughout the village, though, filling every street.

Anything and everything was on sale. Livestock, fresh meat and pungent dried fish, fruits, vegetables, pulses, grains, herbs and medicines, preserves, handmade clothing, household goods and a few luxury items. I noticed that the fresh meat on sale comprised whole pigs, chopped up according to the customer's specifications.

Two women were arguing vehemently about some elementary scales' perceived accuracy. Finally, after some raised voices, the transaction was brought to an amenable solution.

I spent an amusing five minutes watching two old boys attempting to manhandle two hefty old sows into a trailer. They were trying to pull the poor beasts in with their ears and tails. The pigs were having none of it and led the chaps a merry dance. Finally, they managed the job and collapsed in a sweating heap, joining me in laughter as they fought to salvage some sort of dignity. I had thought about helping them but then considered the inevitable consequences of being covered in pig muck, bitten, or both.

Wholesalers were snapping up sacks of grain and loading them onto their trucks. Prospective sellers waited patiently by their stacks of produce, hoping to catch their eye.

I did a complete circuit of the market before grabbing a seat in a sunny spot at a café and ordering a coffee. As soon as I sat down, curious locals surrounded me. I was proving quite a novelty. One old lady was keen to chat, so I had to resort to getting my *Lonely Planet* out and using the vocabulary section at the back. This enabled us to have a conversation of sorts by passing the book backwards and forwards.

Another lady, a stallholder opposite, brought me a big juicy pear and smilingly handed it to me, waving away my offer of payment. It was a lovely interaction with the locals on a memorable day.

The market seemed to get even busier in the afternoon. Many of the men did not seem bothered about making any purchases, leaving that up to their womenfolk, or perhaps they had finished their business earlier. Their focus now seemed on chatting with their friends, swigging rice wine or enjoying snacks from the fast-food vendors, who were doing a roaring trade.

I finally walked back to Duan in the company of scores of villagers laden with their purchases. Or else herding their new livestock acquisitions along the lane. All were seemingly in good humour and chatted together excitedly. The market day expedition indeed seemed to be the social highlight of their week.

I had meant to find someone in town to restitch my boots, which had become a little in need of some needlework, but I had forgotten. The workmanship on my relatively new boots, handcrafted in Hoi An, Vietnam, was probably not of the highest quality they led me to believe was the case. Never mind, I would get the work done in Lijiang.

Occasionally I stopped to admire the scenery, looking up at the majestic peaks embracing this wonderful richly fertile valley. There was by now a sunlit backdrop of a deep azure sky. All the clouds had miraculously disappeared.

I was close to the fictional location of Shangri-La, portrayed in the 1933 novel *Lost Horizon* by Englishman James Hilton. The author described the place in the book as *a mystical, harmonious valley and has become synonymous with any earthly paradise - a sort of Himalayan utopia*. While Lijiang, where I was off to next, claims to be the inspiration for Shangri La, I felt I had found my particular version here.

I stopped along the route to watch some builders working on a house extension for a wealthy-looking man who watched his workers with a close and critical eye. Broad, open red clay tiles were being laid between round, rough-hewn roof timbers. The builders placed other tiles around the lumber and cemented in with a lime and straw mix to create a traditional corrugated roof.

This chap was paying for the best as new walls were being built with locally fired red clay bricks. Other construction work along the route was using old wattle and daub methods, which were probably much cheaper.

As I was enjoying my walk so much in the afternoon sunshine, I went beyond Duan. I took a path following the course of a fast-flowing stream of crystal-clear meltwater. There were sluices at regular intervals where they could draw water off for irrigating the fields.

I sat in the sunshine a little way along, stripping off another layer and watching the workers in the fields coming to the end of their working day.

The sun dipped down behind the mountains quite early and quickly. So, it was back on with the previously discarded clothing, and I was soon retracing my steps to Duan. By the time my hostess served dinner at around 6 pm, it was decidedly chilly, and a multitude of stars twinkled in the inky, still blackness.

The evening passed in the same way as the previous one - there was not a lot of choice. I got Grandma to top up the coals later, read, and listened to the increasingly familiar divas. I also made a dent in the rice wine before getting into my warm and cosy bed.

After breakfast, where I learned hubby had still not returned from Dali, I decided it was time to move on from my little personal Shangri La. I would travel to the place, which was supposedly the real deal in the eyes of many, Lijiang. We would see.

If the man of the household had put in an appearance, there would have been the opportunity of some guided walking up into the foothills, but it was not to be. Que sera, sera. I still felt I had done my visit to this beautiful area justice. So, after settling my modest bill and saying my goodbyes to the family, I trekked off to the main road to await the bus for Lijiang.

Chapter 11

LIJIANG AND THE TIGER LEAPING GORGE

The sun was burning off the early morning mist and melting the small pockets of ground frost as I walked down the lane, exchanging waves with workers in the fields. Then, as I approached the main road, I saw a bus go past, so having missed that one, I walked on for a while.

There were no designated bus stops, so it was simply a matter of flagging a vehicle down when I heard one coming up behind me. It was all very tranquil. Traffic was extremely light, and I felt utterly alone as I walked up the slight incline.

A bus came along soon enough, heading for Jianchuan, where I would need to change for Lijiang. On the outskirts of the town, a pig jam held us up. Many local women were driving stately old sows and their multiple offspring along the road to market. Most behaved and fell readily into line when given a sharp tap with a stick. However, there were a not inconsiderable number of delinquent piglets darting about. They ran in and out of the vehicles and causing general pandemonium. For a good ten minutes, it was mayhem. Oinking and honking squeals from pigs and brakes and shrieks and panicky shouts from the pig ladies who were trying to restore order.

Finally, on reaching the shabby bus station, I found I had to hang around for an hour before my departure. Frankly, I have hung around nicer places, but by 1 pm, I was underway again.

*

The following day I was breakfasting in a beautiful upstairs room in the Old Market cafe in the middle of Lijiang. Highly decorated, carved wooden and brightly painted window shutters on all four sides were open to the fresh mountain air. The old owner, and presumably his son, were at pains to make me comfortable, bringing me coffee, eggs and toast as I looked out onto the thronging crowds below. I was enjoying Lijiang.

It was pretty touristy, but it was also very authentic and in a beautiful location. The town was surrounded by soaring mountains and sitting on a plain 2400 metres above sea level. I was at a height from which I was more used to skiing down pistes in the Alps than wandering around charming ancient cobblestone streets.

The old town, five years earlier in 1997, had been designated UNESCO World Heritage status. It was the best-preserved town in the whole of China and boasted a history of over 1000 years. It had come to prominence on the old horse-tea caravan route, just like Shaxi, from where I had just travelled. But Lijiang was much more extensive and, historically, a more important trading post. The settlement being particularly well-sited close to several key mountain passes.

From my prominent first-floor seat, I had an excellent view of the town. The orange clay-tiled roofs of the old wooden houses and the narrow cobbled streets were so picturesque. Many pretty little stone bridges crossed the network of man-made streams gurgling through the town. I also had a spectacular view of the dominant Jade Dragon Snow Mountain (in reality, a small mountain range) with its thirteen separate peaks glistening pure white. The early morning sun made the snow sparkle and this set dramatically against the cornflower blue sky. The highest crest was a remarkable 5596m or 18,360 feet.

It was mind-blowing to realise I was not that far from Tibet and the mighty peaks of the Himalayas. This breathtaking panorama made me think that, yes, this could indeed be Shangri La for everyone else, although I still had my Shaxi.

Although we only travelled some 80km, the bus journey the previous day took about three hours. The narrow, snaking route climbed and then crossed a plateau. It then quickly started climbing again and never allowed the ancient worn out vehicle I was riding in to build up a head of steam. When we had finally reached Lijiang, I had initially been less than impressed as we first drove through a sizeable metropolis. Scores of major building projects were underway. Just like in so many other Chinese cities I had seen. I later learned, however, that a major earthquake had struck in 1996 and had devastated large swathes of the area. Building work was largely rectifying this earthquake damage.

We had driven on though and finally halted at a far more agreeable place - old town Lijiang. This older part of the city looked totally different. There were wonderful wooden buildings decorated with exotic carvings and red Chinese lanterns. Narrow cobbled streets and a multitude of gurgling watercourses crisscrossing the central district looked intriguing. I couldn't wait to explore the place further. Apparently, the ancient wooden buildings of the old town had withstood the earthquake far more successfully than the more modern buildings in the newer part of town.

A delightful young woman with reasonably good English had spoken to me at the bus depot. Her approach had been a most pleasant change from the usual reception committee. This would normally be a screeching, baying and aggressive mob, mainly of men, all shouting at once about whatever it was they offered. I was immediately in her thrall and allowed myself to be taken to her guesthouse. She gave me the place's name, and I found it had a decent review in *Lonely Planet*. Everything was fine.

Dongba House was a charming old Naxi-style wooden building hundreds of years old. It boasted beautifully carved traditional wooden decorations of flowers and birds around the windows. Naxi was the predominant ethnic grouping in the area, together with the Bai and Yi.

It was not particularly easy to find the place, which was tucked away down a narrow granite street, behind a large full-height wooden gate. It was quite close to the centre, but perhaps tricky to recognise if I didn't concentrate on selecting the right little street. They had basic shared rooms with a loo and shower available at the homestead. The lady in charge allocated me a large ground-floor bedroom that had no evidence of any other guest, so I had struck lucky. Costing just 15 RMB a night with free laundry facilities, it was a snip.

I booked in and dumped my bag on a bed while my new friend waited. She then guided me back the half-mile or so into the centre of town, giving me some helpful information on the way about buses, decent restaurants, tours and trips.

Thanking her kindly for her help, I sent her on her way and enjoyed exploring the enchanting streets. It was a most attractive town, with narrow granite lanes bridging the many leats. These drew water down from higher ponds and were the town's water supply.

I found a cobbler who could restitch my boots while I waited. More exploration led to me finding a popular local's eatery for an evening meal and a couple of beers.

When I had finished my breakfast the next day in the Old Market, I overheard four young travellers in their early thirties. This group had recently come in and was sitting at a corner table discussing Tiger Leaping Gorge. My ears pricked up as I had read about the fabulous gorge and the possibilities of doing a trek. However, I had not fully worked out how to go about booking one.

I introduced myself, and we had a bit of a general traveller's chat, touching on where we had been and where we were going.

"I didn't mean to descend on you like this," I said, "but I overheard you mention the gorge. Are you going on a trek? Where did you book it?" I asked enthusiastically.

"Yeah. We're going tomorrow. You are welcome to come along with us if you would like," the natural group leader, a good-looking, athletic and tanned American called Colin, responded.

"That would be great," I said, and indeed it was an excellent result.

Colin and his equally attractive and tanned girlfriend Suzanne, or Zanne as she liked to be called, were travelling as a couple. They had only recently met up with Drew and Todd (A Kiwi and an Aussie). The two Americans were from Boulder, Colorado, and were keen and experienced climbers and mountaineers. The Rockies being their natural playground.

Having studied the language at university, Colin also benefited from being a fluent speaker of Mandarin. The two Antipodeans were, typical of their ilk, friendly, outgoing young men keen to embrace life. They were a very likeable crew.

It sounded like they had it all worked out, and all I had to do was turn up at the bus stop the next day. We would make the trip independently rather than being part of an organised group. Colin had booked a guesthouse at the start of the walk for the next night before we embarked on the trek the following day. We would stay overnight at a Naxi homestay halfway along the route.

I left the Old Market with a spring in my step in anticipation of the adventure. Further exploration of Lijiang's nooks and crannies and pretty cobbled streets took up the next few hours.

The central area was almost a victim of its own attractiveness, somewhat thronging with visitors. It reminded me of somewhere like Broadway in the Cotswolds, Dinan in France, or perhaps the wonderful little chocolate box village of Gruyere in Switzerland.

There were many Chinese, Korean and Japanese tourists, who all seemed to go in for organised tours. They were happy to follow young Naxi women wearing the full traditional regalia and carrying a banner or flag aloft to guide their group as they meandered through the town.

There were many souvenir shops around the market square, some selling tat. But a lot were displaying quality handmade and embroidered clothing, leatherware and jade jewellery. They seemed to do decent business. Many of the shop owners were entrepreneurial Han who were happy to sell Naxi handiwork.

There were a surprising number of tea shops which also seemed to be popular with visitors. A sign I could decipher outside one such emporium showed I could get a pot of specialist tea for a pretty hefty price. I would need to pay three times what I had spent on my accommodation. I would not be having a cuppa there.

However, everyday town life went on in the way it presumably had for centuries away from the main square. In a smaller courtyard, I came across two Naxi women chatting. One washed clothes and the other vegetables in adjacent large old wooden troughs, and they talked, laughed and joked as they carried out their chores. The washing areas were public facilities fed by a separate running water supply (one for clothes washing and one for food preparation) and drinking water. Using them was just a regular part of their day-to-day life.

I thought back to my washing, which was being done for me by the lady of the house. Earlier in the morning, I was acting the useless dumb male (though perhaps there was not too much acting involved). I was trying to work out how to operate the ancient cold-fill twin tub. The owner came bustling out and took over from me, as I had hoped would happen. She then good-naturedly waved me away, showing that she would have it all done by my return. Excellent.

Further along from the ladies who were doing their laundry, was a busy market where Naxi wives were stocking up with fresh produce. Walking to the edge of town and out into the countryside, I enjoyed the sunshine and gazing up at the beautiful and awe-inspiring grandeur of the lofty mountain peaks.

After making a circuit around some rural lanes, I went back and found Dongba House. My washing was dry, when I checked back so I folded it up, and put it away. I then popped back into town for an early evening beer, which I thought I deserved.

Later, I treated myself to a leisurely Italian meal at an upmarket central restaurant by the main square. It was a little incongruous to find such a place in the middle of rural China, I felt, but most enjoyable.

As I was dining, I saw a group of Naxi women of all ages, from pre-teens to grandmothers, all in traditional dress, gather in the square. With a trio of men providing some instrumental support, they performed a range of elegant and time-honoured dance moves. There were no tourists around at this time of the evening. I was sure the ladies were simply dancing for their pleasure and practice rather than for tips. It honoured me to watch their display as I sipped my chilled dry white wine from my seat on the restaurant terrace.

Just before 8.30 the next morning, I was at the designated bus stop to meet up with my trekking gang.

The first part of the journey was out to the little town of Qiaotou. This is now more commonly known as Hutiaoxia Town, translated as Tiger Leaping Gorge Town, some 60km north of Lijiang.

Having reached Qiaotou without incident, and after a coffee break, we (Colin really) negotiated with a local taxi driver. The bloke agreed on the fare for taking us out to Tina's Guesthouse, which was going to be our base for the evening. His vehicle was an old minibus, with more than a few scrapes and dents on the bodywork.

There was not a lot to Qiaotou; it was just a ribbon of dilapidated, dusty old wooden buildings straggled out down the main road. Most were catering to the burgeoning trekking, adventure and backpacker market.

The route was about 25 km via what had been, until comparatively recently, a mere mule track clinging to the mountainside. Even as we edged cautiously along, passing places were being hacked out of the sheer rock sides by gangs of workers just using picks and shovels. At a couple of other sections, workers were clearing away a recent landslip that had covered the road. At another point, a vast chunk of what had recently been the road had disappeared down the steep escarpment.

I was in the front seat, so I had a bird's-eye and vertigo-inducing view of how tight the road was. Rocky slopes down to the foaming milky-turquoise Jinsha river, some 500m below, were scarily precipitous. The river was called the Jinsha here but would soon metamorphose into the mighty Yangtze.

Our nonchalant driver, one hand on the wheel, half turning to chat to Colin in his native tongue, obviously knew what he was doing, but it was pretty petrifying. Waterfalls dissected the highway, tumbling down from on high, making passage even more perilous. I had to use a lot of willpower to put the potential dangers of the challenging route to the back of my mind and focus on the breath-taking scenery.

After the best part of an hour, we all disembarked from the old minibus. We were all relieved and happy to be at our destination, and headed down the steep path to the guesthouse. This was a pleasant enough sprawling wooden building that was dwarfed by the landscape. I think we were all rather pleased to be trekking back to Qiaotou and would not need to take that road again by minibus.

The amazingly scenic gorge, is one of the largest in the world. With Jade Dragon Snow Mountain to the south of us and Haba Snow Mountain behind us to the north, we were in a truly spectacular region. Both these peaks top out at over 5500m above sea level and Tiger Leaping Gorge is a 3790m yawning chasm at its deepest. The canyon gained its legendary name from a mythical tiger who leapt the 25m wide river via a boulder mid-stream to evade its pursuers.

We were currently some 500m above the river, and Colin, as the natural group leader, intended we take the 50-minute trek down (and back up again). Once we had completed the booking formalities, we would head off. The eponymous Tina welcomed us into her humble but spacious guesthouse and allocated the rooms. The other four shared, but I, the latecomer, secured a large bedroom to myself, which was more than acceptable.

It was then time to take the tricky path down to the Jinsha, guided by a handmade sketch map. Tina's was directly above 'the middle rapids' section of the gorge. In the opposite direction, over the other side of the road, was the steep path climbing up to the 'high route.' We would set off up here the next day to meet the upper path, which ran some twenty-odd kilometres back to Tiger Leaping Gorge Town.

For now, it was down to the river. The path initially, whilst quite steep and narrow, was acceptably manageable, and we made steady progress. It became decidedly tricky a little later on, and even a mountain goat might have looked a little askance if required to navigate the twisting narrow trail.

They had gouged a slab of rock out of a sheer cliff at one exciting section, leaving a half-metre wide path to negotiate. Directly below us was a straight hundred-metre drop to the roaring, raging torrents below.

Colin and Zanne danced through whilst the rest of the party was decidedly more circumspect. Not to say in imminent danger of an unplanned bowel evacuation.

As we continued to negotiate the trail with considerable care and get closer to the river, the roar and power of the water was quite unbelievable. The mighty surge of white water smashed through the canyon with remarkable ferocity.

They have categorised the Jinsha as unnavigable. Although some intrepid rafters tried to descend the route some years' previously. No one ever saw them again.

We finally reached the river. There were beautiful water-eroded giant boulders in midstream. It was possible to pick a route carefully from one huge rock to another and become at one with the river.

It was quite a surreal moment when Zanne, on a large, smooth and flattish midstream monolith, practised her yoga moves. Not to be outdone, Colin found a mid-rapids location for a spot of serious rock climbing as well.

We were all taken aback by the tremendous force of nature surrounding us. We spent a long time, quietly and individually, appreciating the almost spiritual atmosphere in this granite-walled cathedral. The tumultuous maelstrom crashed through the gorge at the start of its epic 3,900-mile journey.

In the wet season, the waters would be four or five metres higher. The water-gouged smoothness of the rock up to those sorts of heights showed the high water mark.

After a beautiful and dreamlike period down by the river, we trekked back up, with three of us not overly keen on renegotiating that narrow, tricky section. The difficult bit out of the way, though, we almost skipped home. We were looking forward to a beer or two, a home-cooked meal and the chance to get to know each other more.

We had already bonded nicely as a group and fell into easy conversation as we opened up a beer or two while waiting for our meal. As night fell and visits to the outside loo became necessary, we all commented about the star-spangled but otherwise fabulous jet-black sky with virtually zero light pollution. The planets, comets and even artificial satellites, as well as the multitude of stars put on a magnificent celestial display for us to enjoy.

We enjoyed a wholesome and satisfying meal together, downed a few more beers and chatted about a wide range of topics. We also played several games of cards before retiring to dream about the next day's trekking.

After a decent and sustaining breakfast comprising eggs and lots of fruits and grains, we headed off at around 10. It was a calm, sunny day.

The first couple of hours were a strenuous, steep, constantly brutal assault to reach the high path. This first section caused the thighs to burn, and we needed regular breaks to relax and catch our breath in the thin air.

However, it importantly allowed us all to look back down at the speck that was Tina's homestead. And much further below, see the icy white water of the Jinsha coursing through the bottom of the gorge.

Above and beyond the river, we could see over to Jade Mountain. Turning to face the way we were walking, the white-tipped Haba Snow Mountain presided majestically over the landscape.

Luckily, a little while later, we could discern the red markings on boulders almost hidden by foliage that showed that we had reached the high path. We would now trek across the slope rather than continue climbing. Taking an old miner's route, we were almost suspended in mid-air halfway between the river and the mountain peaks.

It was enjoyable walking, with a mix of slope and terrain and fabulous views in all directions. Taking in great lungfuls of clean, crisp mountain air to fuel our progress felt marvellous. We all appreciated our good fortune to be out in such wonderfully benign conditions. Just the five of us in that vast mountain wilderness - we had not seen another soul since leaving Tina's.

We made good steady progress and stopped at the Halfway House because it was there rather than for any need to take a break. However, we all appreciated the opportunity for a coffee on the upper balcony. This rustic seating area commanded extensive views of the gorge and the mountains and was indeed a moment to savour.

One particular highlight of this idyllic refuge was the toilet. Screened off for modesty, but otherwise open to the elements, it was definitely a facility with a spectacular outlook. One of Michael Palin's later travelogues featured this 'loo with a view'.

So, onwards and upwards, and indeed downwards, we continued our trek, seeing only a few other walkers and the odd local shepherd.

Soon after our pit stop, we reached a demanding steep uphill section where they had hacked a track out of the rock face. Sheer drops lay to the side and there was the added difficulty of negotiating waterfalls and narrow, slippery wooden bridges.

After this came a very steep lengthy climb through forests which tested the heart, lungs and limbs. This testing section had us all appreciating the effect of the altitude on the body's ability to deal with the challenges we faced.

With burning thighs and screaming lungs, we eventually topped out. Then we began the '28 bends' section, a descent down to the Naxi guesthouse that was to be our resting place for the night.

We had made good progress and probably could have gone all the way to Quiaotu, but there was no point. It was not a competition after all - we were there to enjoy the mountains, the physical effort and the camaraderie. There was no rush.

At about 5.30 in the afternoon, we dragged ourselves across the threshold of the Naxi family guesthouse, booking arranged courtesy of Colin. The lady of the house gave us a wonderfully warm welcome and immediately provided tea and snacks.

The place was like the Bai house I had stayed at a few days earlier. It had a central courtyard accessed via a fine full height and wide ancient timber door. The building was surrounded by domestic accommodation on three sides and barns on the other. Again, this was a working farm, and with Colin doing an excellent job interpreting, we gleaned that the family had only been taking trekking guests in for a year.

After a beer and a rest, we four males felt sufficiently re-energised to grab the racquets and shuttles lying around. We took to the badminton court set up in the middle of the courtyard for an impromptu game.

Then some more beers, cards, a substantial and much-appreciated meal, followed by more beers and card games meant for a most enjoyable evening.

After a good night's sleep and a leisurely breakfast, we were ready to complete our journey into Hutiaoxia Town. I remember breakfast included some corn soup with the consistency of wallpaper paste, which was perhaps an acquired taste.

The terrain was a little easier than the previous day. As we knew we did not have a considerable distance to go, we all settled into a steady pace and made sure that we enjoyed the last miles.

Once in town, Colin again came to the fore, bargaining with a local minibus operator to take us back to Lijiang rather than going by public bus. We all considered this to be a sound idea, and the outcome was that this approach was not much more costly, and we halved the journey time.

Once I had realised that Lijiang had a new airport, I decided I would take a short internal flight south to Jinghong. I would be on my way back to Laos, then Thailand, and eventually to Bangkok and home. So, getting to Lijiang by early afternoon allowed me to organise my booking for a flight the next day.

The gang had all agreed to meet up for a post-trek meal and celebratory drinks that evening in an atmospheric old place off the market square. We had all got on really well and had enjoyed each other's company. Hence, we spent a most convivial final evening together, swapping tales and discussing plans and ideas for further travel adventures as well as general hopes and ambitions for the future. Tiger Leaping Gorge had truly been a wonderful, shared, and memorable experience.

Chapter 12

JINGHONG AND ESCAPING CHINA

At the crack of dawn, or close to it, I walked through central Lijiang. The street cleaners were out in force, children made their way to school for a long day of study, and the dim sum vendors fired up their steamers in readiness for another day's business.

I found where the airport courtesy bus stopped and was soon on my way to the gleaming new terminal building. The 1000-kilometre journey passed quickly, and another complimentary minibus swiftly dropped me in downtown Jinghong. The airport was conveniently very close to the city centre.

Being in the tropics in the far south of the Yunnan province and at a lower altitude than the mountainous plateau where Lijiang sat, the weather was much warmer and muggier than I had recently experienced.

Walking through the somnolent palm-fringed boulevards seeking suitable accommodation, I realised not a lot seemed to be going on. It was mid-morning by now, but there was little traffic around. The place seemed to have a distinctly soporific, 'can't be bothered', 'manana will do' vibe about it.

There were small groups of old men playing mah jong together in the shade, and shop girls sat outside their empty boutiques smoking and drinking coffee from paper cups distractedly. A couple of supposed delivery men were lying prone on the grass, dozing in the sunshine, but that was about it.

There was considerable evidence that the city had undergone the recent and extensive redevelopment programme I had witnessed in many places throughout my visit to China. White-tiled concrete boxes from the 'inside-out public convenience' style of architecture so prevalent in China were replacing beautiful traditional wooden homes.

There were several smart new hotels, but I could not seem to locate any cheaper backpacker-type places. Taking a side road, I had more luck. After rejecting a couple of very shabby and downright unsanitary places, I came across a wonderful old centrally located hotel. They offered me an excellent self-contained room with all mod cons for a very reasonable 20 yen or 'kwai', as they seemed to refer to the currency here.

Divesting myself of my rucksack, I changed into shorts and sandals. It was warm, sunny and tropical weather, and sauntered off to see what Jinghong offered.

Random strolling brought me out to the new crossing over the Mekong I had spotted earlier. This construction was an impressive piece of civil engineering; a concrete bridge suspended on steel cables from a high central pillar. Walking on to, but not over, the route for a better view, I contemplated going to the opposite bank. As there did not seem to be much of any interest on the other side, I returned to town. I had though spotted some extensive new buildings on the riverside a couple of hundred metres away,

The waters were low, the slow trickle of the muddy river here in sharp contrast to the powerful surging of the Jinsha we had all witnessed a couple of days earlier. There was little evidence of any commercial river traffic.

I wandered back into town and found Zhuanghong Lu, a street lined with dozens of Burmese jade shops. Here, smiling sarong-clad

Burmese ladies were far more energised and entrepreneurial than the Han or Dai shopkeepers (Dai was the predominant minority ethnic grouping in the area.)

While the Dai people were predominant in the area, there are significant numbers of other minority groupings, such as the Yi, Wa, Hmong, and Naxi. This is a region where the ubiquitous Han are nowhere near as prevalent as elsewhere in China.

I was not in the market for jade but could admire their business-like approach in trying to secure a sale. They would lure in unsuspecting tourists with the offer of a chair and a cold drink. They would then mesmerise them with their smooth and well-practiced sales patter, extolling the virtues of unique pieces of the ornamental mineral.

There were also a few shifty characters along the street trying to sell more exotic and illegal substances. I gave them a wide berth.

In the evening, I found that the friendly and quite new-looking Mekong Café was the place to be. Enthusiastic and attentive staff, cold beer, splendid music and decent food was my conclusion. An extensive area of squishy, comfortable seating on the veranda made it very easy to linger for a while after dining.

I should have moved on the following day, but didn't get around to it. Perhaps Jinghong's torpor was affecting me. My loose plan was to get to Laos to explore the country further and then move on to Chiang Mai, my adopted home base in northern Thailand. I was keen to find an alternative to bus travel and believed there was a possibility of getting down the Mekong. The low water levels which I had seen first hand made me reconsider this option.

The next day I thought I would look into the possibility of boat travel more rigorously, and this time walked right across the modernistic bridge to the new buildings I had spotted earlier. These turned out to be the river port buildings. This extensive development had signage in English and Chinese. There were substantial waiting rooms for passengers, gleaming new toilet facilities, enquiry desks, ticket offices, and customs and immigration points. But it was like the Marie Celeste - no one was home.

Eventually, I spotted a young lad, who I took to be a Boy Scout, but in fact, was a fully fledged customs officer. We had a tricky conversation, as will be the case when neither understands a word of the other's language. However, I gleaned from him that boats were not leaving Jinghong at this time of the year. With the state of the river, this was pretty obvious.

A more mature female officer then joined us. She brusquely demanded my passport. I meekly handed my document over, and she disappeared into the bowels of the building.

As I hung around, not being able to do much else, a young Thai man appeared. After confirming that it was not possible to take a boat from Jinghong, he offered the nugget that it was viable, further downstream from Guang Lai Port. From this second port, he assured me, I could get a boat down to Laos and Thailand.

I could not find the place marked on my *Lonely Planet* map, but he pointed out exactly where it was, on the Mekong. At the point where the noble river left China on its endless journey down to its ultimate destination, the vast delta area in southern Vietnam. Beyond the Chinese border, it was Myanmar on the west, and Laos on the east.

By this time, wearing a self-satisfied smile, the female customs official had returned. She handed me back my freshly stamped passport theatrically. With it, she also handed over a sealed letter with lots of Chinese lettering on the envelope and a separate note in English. She forcefully clarified that I must hand the letter in at border control at Ma Mu Shi.

I thanked her for her efforts and considered that was the matter over, not realising what hassle this passport stamping and the acceptance of the letter would bring.

I went back into town and tried all three bus stations to see how I could get to Guang Lai, which was to be my favoured option, but drew a complete blank. So, I resorted to my original idea of going to Mohan by bus and onwards into Laos.

I worked out where and when I could get a bus to Mengla the next day. It was impossible to reach Mohan in one hit, and with my brain hurting from all the logistical considerations, I retired to the Mekong Café for the evening.

The following day, after an enjoyable and mellow soiree at my favourite Jinghong watering hole, I walked through the misty morning streets to catch the 7.40 bus to Mengla. The journey was only 190 kilometres but could take between four and seven hours.

As had become my familiar tactic, I commandeered the back seat of the fifteen-seater vehicle. I settled down as we crossed the river. We immediately wound our way up the hills beyond the valley.

Soon, the road deteriorated to a shambolic, rutted, potholed track, and the bus lurched, swayed and bounced along at not much more than a walking pace. The journey was going to be a matter of endurance; that much was obvious. All I could do was accept my fate and try to enjoy the passing scenery of virgin tropical forests and spectacular mountains the best I could. The luxuriant, dense green foliage featuring giant ferns, stands of bamboo, and various palms was apparently home to some quite exotic wildlife. None put in an appearance for me.

There were occasional dust-covered thatch and bamboo villages along the way, with small patches of subsistence cropping and rice paddies. More commercially sized rubber plantations were spotted, but mostly it was dense jungle. The road surface improved to a degree, though, and the driver could touch down in Mengla in exactly four hours, which I deemed a commendable effort.

I walked the mile down the scruffy main street from the bus depot and out the other side to get to the southern terminus. From here, I hoped to continue my journey to Mohan. An open-air restaurant at the bus station provided an excellent point and pick lunch. Then, I found a driver with a minibus that could take me to Mohan. But I needed to hang around while he tried to drum up more trade.

After about forty minutes, the driver accepted he would not attain a full complement of passengers for this trip, and we set off around half full.

Jinghong and Escaping China

*

A little over twenty-four hours later, I knocked the cap off a cold beer, enjoying the reassuring hiss that escaped from the bottle and glugged the amber nectar into my glass. I adjusted myself in my hammock and contemplated the vagaries of unstructured travel. The highs and lows and the sheer frisson of excitement produced by the anticipation of what was in store around every corner.

I was on the starboard stern of the *'Ja Long Shing'*; a 40 m-long Laos-registered general cargo vessel bound for Chiang Saen in Northern Thailand. China rapidly receded into the distance as we made swift progress down the fast-flowing yellowy-brown Mekong. Myanmar was on the starboard bow, Laos to port.

From Mengla the previous day, the minibus had rattled along for an hour and a half before reaching the nondescript border post of Mohan. There I had planned to cross into Laos and then take a bus to Nam Tha. That did not happen.

The youthful (the officials all seemed to be very young) customs officer was pleasant enough as I handed over my passport and the accompanying letter.

Then, in halting English and smiling continuously, he said,

"You have big problem."

Explaining clearly how I came to have my passport stamped in Jinghong and why I had the official letter, I tried to reason with him. Telling him I could not find Guang Lai Port and that I aimed to cross the border here. Why was it a problem? My passport and a new visa were in order. What was the issue?

"You have big problem," he repeated, still, annoyingly, smiling.

It was surely not a big problem in the grand scheme of things, I reiterated. My documentation was correct; all he had to do was let me through the border.

An attempt at acting out him erasing the offending mark and over-stamping the document was not well received. He, most seriously and earnestly, got across to me that the authorities would deem such an action treasonable.

As I did not wish to spend time in some labour camp in Outer Mongolia, I dropped this proposal rapidly.

"It is not your fault," he said reasonably.

"I know," I replied, becoming quite frustrated.

"So I shouldn't have to suffer the consequences."

My analysis did not wash. I appealed to the junior official to speak to a superior, to no avail. He was adamant. I could not leave China at this border crossing.

I had to find Ma Mu Shu somehow, as prescribed in the letter.

Annoyingly, I had exchanged my remaining Chinese currency with a money changer on the street earlier, receiving a brick-sized chunk of Kip in return. So I had no Chinese money. The money changers had now disappeared from the road, and there was no Bank of China (the only exchange bank) in town.

Finally, I had to grovel with an autocratic jobsworth at another bank. This bumptious official eventually deigned to exchange $15 US from my reserve stash at a highly unattractive rate (for me, that was). I did not get the normal exchange advice slip, so this unsavoury, balding, middle-aged chancer had duped both his employers and me to make a tidy personal profit. But at least I now had a little cash.

I then had a minibus trip back to Mengla, from where I needed to find out where the hell Ma Mu Shu was and how I could get there. I was presuming the place was the same as Mamushi that I found on the map, but which appeared to be at least 25km from the border.

Buses had finished for the night by the time we reached Mengla. My increasingly tatty *Lonely Planet* guide described the tiny settlement as "just a small town trying to find something to do on a Saturday night". That seemed to sum the place up, and here I was, on a Saturday night and of necessity, eager to embrace its charms.

I booked into a shabby little hotel and the owner allocated me a reasonable double room. The ablutions, however, were extremely basic, communal, and open to the elements. It was not exactly the Ritz.

Whilst my expectations were not high, I found a friendly little place for a meal. I pointed at various ingredients in plastic bowls and had a spicy personalised stir fry rustled up for me by the lady of the house. Some freshly roasted and salted peanuts and a couple of beers finished things off nicely. The cook's teenage daughter hovered around me, smiling coyly, which was a little disconcerting.

Later I was walking the streets seeking signs of life when I came across a first-floor open-air bar. A buzz of conversation and occasional hoots of laughter drifted down to street level. I investigated and soon fell in with a couple of German girls studying in China and a young Mancunian lad I had bumped into on my earliest minibus trip of the day.

We shared a couple of rounds of drinks, and then a succession of locals joined us. They realised the girls could speak Chinese, one of them being exceptionally proficient. The locals loved the idea of speaking in their language with a westerner, so it ended up being a lively and highly sociable evening.

Various people frustratingly directed me to all three of the town's bus stations at some stage in the morning. Eventually, being assured it was the right bus, I boarded my connection to the mysterious Mamushi and paid my 15 RMB fare. It wasn't the right bus.

A couple of hours of the usual rattling and bumping around later, it dropped me off at some godforsaken place in the middle of nowhere. On the scale of one-horse towns, this one didn't rate half a donkey.

A grand total of 3 RMB in cash was in my wallet; Exactly where I was, I did not know. There was no sign of a river, and I was not at a border crossing. My next move was something I contemplated. Perhaps an intensive short course in spoken Chinese?

A clump of locals who had gathered around me debated my predicament. The noisy conclusion was that I needed to go,

"That way," accompanied by lots of pointing up a distant hill.

They summoned a motorbike taxi and as his required fare was 3 RMB, I went along with the hare-brained scheme. The chap took me a few miles and then deposited me at a dusty crossroads in the middle of a hamlet of half a dozen buildings. A village council and a bunch of assorted raggy children suddenly appeared to discuss my next move. The conclusion seemed to be that I needed to go up a red dirt track for about 40km - there was a bus due in a couple of hours.

A woman manning a pair of woks sat on burners gestured to me to see if I needed food. I had not eaten all day, so the answer was yes, but I now only had dollars. She was not happy with dollars, so she put the food on hold. A shopkeeper was also reluctant to change dollars, but an amiable chap of about sixty sauntered up and offered me 10 RMB for a dollar. So I cashed in the two single dollar bills I had.

The wok lady readily appreciated my improved cash liquidity. Getting fed became an option again, and she started fussing about preparing some noodle soup for me.

I had just finished my lunch when a bus rolled up to stop right by us. The villagers all confirmed that this indeed was the bus I needed, and so I was off again.

We rattled along, creating vast clouds of red dust for a couple of hours before the driver indicated I should get out and also pay him 10 RMB. Not obviously a border place, the village had a river, but it was not where I needed to be. Another gang of villagers gathered around to debate my predicament.

A bus appeared, and I showed the driver my letter. He was very positive, nodding vigorously and saying,

"Yes. Yes."

I got on, and we headed back the way I had come. This turn of events did not look promising. However, a few miles down the trail, we turned at a junction. I was pleased to see we were now driving down a different route and one that I had not travelled previously.

We drove on for an hour or more, passing through dusty hamlets of bamboo and thatch shacks. Descending into a wide valley, we then reached a new wide tarmac road with a cluster of modern white-tiled buildings. We stopped, and some passengers got out, but the driver gestured for me to stay put. He still seemed confident. I was less than convinced.

We drove a short way down the empty road before he brought his vehicle to a standstill by a sparkling new white building with the sign CUSTOMS above the door. Smiling broadly, the driver pointed to the sign. I thanked him and gave him my last remaining RMB, which included a small tip.

Chapter 13

NEITHER HERE NOR THERE

After all the hassles of the last few hours, what happened next was amazing. I went into the customs office and asked the guy at the desk whether he spoke English. He didn't, but went to fetch his superior officer. A charming and courteous man of around forty came out from a back office and, taking my proffered passport and letter, asked how he could help. He checked the documents and returned them to me with a smile, saying,

"These are all in order."

I then said I wanted to take a boat to Laos or Thailand, but I was not holding my breath, realising that it was improbable.

"This man is leaving right now," he replied.

He was gesturing to a young Chinese man standing at the back of the room in tailored shorts and a collared short-sleeved white shirt. Clutching a briefcase, he strode over to join us.

I repeated my request, and he readily agreed.

"Yes, I can take you as far as Chiang Saen in Thailand."

I quickly checked my map and found the place was just down from the Golden Triangle where Thailand, Myanmar and Laos meet.

I thought that would do nicely.

"That would be very good, thank you."

I established the journey would take twenty-four hours and would cost a not unreasonable 200 RMB. The slight problem, of course, was my zero holdings of the said currency.

Being a man of the world, the boat owner said he would accept dollars and used quickly took his calculator from the briefcase. He came up with the figure of $24 at the official conversion rate. I was most grateful and counted out the cash.

We then, accompanied by the helpful customs officer, went out of the back of the building and, descending a ridge, came to a concrete quayside. Half a dozen vessels 30m to 40m in length were waiting for departure at the rudimentary dock.

The owner pointed out a dark green boat, tidier than any of the others, with a two-storey block at the stern housing the cabins, mess and bridge. Empty cargo holds ran down the full length to the bow. The pleasing-looking vessel was the *'Ja Long Shing'*.

I clambered up the gangway and onto the deck, where a young customs officer was finishing checking the crews' papers. Wanting to make some sort of statement to emphasise his status and show off his command of English, he officiously ordered me to stand and present my passport; I did as I was told with due deference. I had met his sort before - many times. He accepted the document after he had given it a cursory inspection. Grunting, he passed it back to me and was on his way.

A crew member showed me to my berth, which was a spacious cabin on the starboard bow. Completely built from steel, it comprised a wide bed, a built-in table and chair, a loo and shower and plentiful storage. The cabin also had panoramic windows to the front and the side. It was perfect. From what I could make out, I was the only passenger on the voyage.

The engines fired into life, and we pulled out into the mainstream. Moving to the stern where there was a hammock set up on a bit of open deck, I made myself comfortable. I thought I might as well make use of it.

It would be a wonderful trip; watching the scenery passing by in comfort on a boat was a much better option. A far better option than being blinded and suffocated by dust in a battered old bus with minimal suspension.

I watched the helmsman's early manoeuvres and thought that these riverboats must have a very shallow draft. I could see the river had treacherous rocks breaking through the water at regular intervals. There were also long sections of rapids to be negotiated looming in the middle distance.

The skipper had more than a tricky job on his hands. With all the swells and eddies, the tightness of the bends and the fast-flowing Mekong itself, navigation required considerable skill and much concentration. I hoped he was competent, and his early handling of the vessel showed he appeared to be so. He lined the cargo boat up, using the river as a white water slalom canoeist would, to get into the optimum position to negotiate the safest passage. Constantly changing the engine speed and throwing his rudder around to swing the long ship to where he wanted it, we made it through sections of white water shallows.

As the sun sank into the western sky, I went back to my cabin. A few minutes later, I had cause to adjust my assessment of the skipper's boat management skills. There was an almighty crash and the sound of screeching metal on unforgiving rock as the boat went from 20 knots to zero in a split second. A nanosecond later, there came the sound of collateral damage in the galley as pots, pans, and crockery smashed.

I raced down to the stern, where the poor middle-aged Chinese lady who had been in the middle of preparing dinner was looking decidedly befuddled. Scalding water had burnt her arm, but fortunately not seriously. She had also sliced open her hand, bashed her head and suffered a thick lip. I sat her down as crew members came in to help. We patched her up, and all sorted out the mess of broken crockery, glass and boxes of dried goods and salvaged most of the dinner.

In the meantime, the ship's engine shrieked as the vessel was reversed off the rocks. The helmsman then deliberately drove the bow into a sandbank to where the crew could check for any leaks or significant damage. A comprehensive check revealed two deep indentations in the hull, but no penetration below the waterline. We had been lucky.

It was now dark, so we trundled on cautiously for a little while before finding somewhere safe to tie up for the night.

The chef had recovered her composure, and rescued dinner and they gave me the call to join the crew for our evening meal. Someone handed me a beer (luckily only a couple of bottles had smashed in the accident), and I sat down for some welcome food. The crew were chatty and amiable, and, considering the language difficulties, I joined in the banter and laughter as much as possible.

The food was basic but plentiful with lots of spicy fried vegetables and rice and some pre-chewed gristle, which I gave a miss. There was some fresh fruit as dessert.

After dinner, the crew played a noisy game of cards, and I took a second beer back to my cabin to read for a while. There was no sign of the owner, which was probably as well, considering the crash. I had seen him get off on the Myanmar bank the previous afternoon, complete with his briefcase, before the accident. He visited an official-looking shack flying the national flag but had not seen him return.

I awoke the following day as we got underway at around 8 am. After some tricky manoeuvring, an hour later, we berthed alongside three other similar-sized boats. There were also half a dozen smaller craft at a seemingly newly built concrete wharf.

We were at the Burmese bank and stayed there all morning. Crewmen were busy unloading various items of cargo into a posse of waiting trucks from the vessels in front of us in the queue.

Fit-looking men showing both strength and agility made multiple journeys to move the cargo by hand. These young stevedores, balancing carefully, raced up and down the gangplanks tirelessly all day to get the job done.

As the sun broke through the morning mist, I struck up a conversation with a young Thai woman on the adjacent vessel who spoke good English. She was from Chiang Rai in Northern Thailand. I knew the city. They were on their way to the port of Guang Lai (which I never found) where she had a job acting as a guide for some Thai tourists.

"We will be here all day." she reckoned.

This proved to be correct. The journey would not be a twenty-four-hour trip.

Fortunately, time was not a problem for me, and I was enjoying the entire experience, but it would be nice to know when I might be finally disembarking - and where. I was still entertaining thoughts about exploring Laos, although I was also considering I might go back to Thailand. We would see.

I went to get my new friend a coffee from the galley, and we continued to chat. She introduced me to a tall, pony-tailed Chinese man. He was her friend and travelling companion. He didn't look delighted with life, and as we had no shared language, we just nodded before he disappeared again.

The girl explained he was down in the dumps as two of the six fighting cocks he was travelling with had died the previous day because of the heat in the hold. The remaining four, I could see in bamboo cages, now on the open deck, seemed okay. But his loss was a significant financial blow, as these specially bred and highly trained creatures were much prized.

Li, as my new acquaintance was called, then told me about other trading activities that regularly occurred on the banks of the Mekong. On both sides of the river, there were many illicit drug factories hidden in the dense jungle. These illegal manufacturing operations were prolific. They produced a range of opium and heroin derivatives, amphetamines and cannabis products. A considerable army of traders and smugglers worked in their distribution.

Just before lunch, one ship slipped away from its moorings, and we slotted into its place.

We ate lunch in the mess room whilst a truck fully laden with four-metre-long logs arrived. These were to be part of our cargo.

After lunch, the Burmese labourers got to work prising logs from the truck. Rolling them to the quayside and then down planks onto the ship from they dropped them into our hold. The constant thunderous racket of these massive chunks of timber falling into the steel hold was too much for me. So I decided I would take myself off for a walk. There were still a few hours of loading to be undertaken.

I was, I supposed, an illegal alien, as although I had a visa I had not officially entered the country, anyway, I went walkabout in Myanmar.

I walked up the road leading away from the quay for a couple of kilometres before reaching a little fly-blown village of very basic bamboo and palm leaf homes. Scrawny chickens scratched in the dust and mangy cats and dogs slept in the sunshine.

Initially, there was no sign of any human life. However, I shortly came across a couple of bemused locals tending their vegetable stall, shocked at seeing a European in their village. The old man recovered his poise, smiled and, as he could see I had been walking for a while in the fierce afternoon heat, offered me a glass of water. He took pains to show that the water was indeed potable, and that he had boiled it, and I thanked him.

I walked on for a while, but there was little of interest, just endless miles of dense jungle, so I doubled back.

Nearing the riverside, another logging truck overtook me and watched as, in the distance, it pulled up in front of the *'Ja Long Shing'*. We were obviously taking another load on board.

The noise was not as bad now as timber fell onto other logs rather than into the empty metal hold. I tried to block it from my mind and got away as far as possible from the noise. Spreading my sleeping bag out on the flat steel roof above the bridge and laying in the sun reading for the rest of the afternoon was ideal.

The unloading of this second vehicle took until about 7 pm, making it clear we would stay overnight.

We dined on the usual fare, had a couple of beers, laughed and joked, and I then left the crew to their cards and retired to my cabin. It quickly became very hushed.

The sound of thunder came crashing into my dream in the early hours, and I was wide awake in an instant. After about ten minutes, the thunder subsided to be replaced by a most spectacular show of sheet lightning. It was like something out of a Hammer Horror movie, with the entire sky to the north illuminated like daylight as flashes came in swift succession.

Up to now, there had been no rain, but then a few heavy drops fell, and the crew emerged noisily to spread tarpaulins over the cargo. They just about got the job done as I watched out of my front window. Then, a sudden wind rushed down the valley, heralding an almighty downpour, and they scuttled away as the heavens opened.

I went up to the upper deck for a better view of the fabulous celestial pyrotechnics. Opposite, the hills were almost jumping out in the mega-watt brightness of the lightning and the rain coming down in epic proportions. The rain seemed to ebb and flow for a while, but then suddenly, the torrents reached a mega-crescendo lasting for ten minutes before relenting slightly. Early morning the crew was up to empty the huge puddles that had formed on the sagging tarps.

The storm had not cleared the atmosphere, which was still very humid and the sky murky with wispy low clouds obscuring the hills opposite. A weak imitation of its previous day's incarnation, the sun had put in a late appearance.

As I waited for what I assumed to be the off, the crew came out under instruction to remove the tarpaulin from the final third of the hold. This was in readiness for loading a cargo of tobacco in hessian sacks from the adjacent ship. The Burmese labour force had miraculously reappeared to do the heavy lifting work, and I noticed we were getting decidedly lower in the water by this stage.

On the riverbank, by the dock, a smart black saloon and a Ford 4x4 suddenly appeared. Men got out from each vehicle, delved into briefcases and concluded some business, swapping paperwork and bundles of cash. I didn't recognise either of the men from a distance. However, one was probably my original benefactor. Having only met him briefly, I would have had some trouble recognising him now.

A group of four bare-breasted and shoeless Akha women appeared around this time, looking to sell bundles of vegetables. It seemed we did not need their produce, and they trudged off disconsolately. Quite a bizarre and unexpected incident from my point of view.

Tarpaulins finally in place over the tobacco, we got underway. The stretch of the Mekong immediately downriver from the quay looked to me to be distinctly tricky to navigate. The river had narrowed to about two boat widths approaching two fearsome-looking tall rocky outcrops. It then swung around first to the right, then to the left through some treacherous white water.

We were stern downstream, so we headed up the river for a kilometre, where the skipper deliberately ran the ship into a sandbank on the Laos side. A hefty stake was sledge-hammered into the sand by a member of the crew and a hawser put around it. The helmsman then tried to spin the boat around on its axis so that we were facing downstream. Unfortunately, we were stuck deep into the sandbank and needed to redistribute some cargo to give us clearance.

The dapper little skipper came down to organise proceedings, and the crew got on with moving the tobacco sacks from the bow to the stern holds. I helped in this endeavour, treating the episode as a bit of a workout. We manhandled some tons of cargo for over half an hour before finally being able to refloat the vessel.

After a hasty lunch, we swung the ship around with no problem. We were on our way again and facing the correct way down the Mekong.

With the heavily laden vessel already having water lapping at the gunwales, we now had the narrow section of rapids to negotiate. Soon we were through the narrow gap, the skipper revving up and then throttling back to take the optimum line as we rode the rapids skilfully. I had been white water rafting previously, but never in a 40 m-long steel-hulled cargo ship fully loaded with timber and tobacco. It was a bit of a surreal experience.

The skipper did an excellent job of getting us through this challenging section without further incident. We then enjoyed a period of cruising down a broader, more benign section of the river.

We pulled in at a wide beach area on the Laos bank a little later. As far as I could make out, the sole purpose of this unscheduled stop was negotiating the purchase of a recently shot deer offered for sale by an entrepreneurial villager. He was asking too much, though - it was a dear deer - and we continued our journey without a supply of fresh meat. A pity I would have enjoyed a lovely fresh venison steak for dinner.

It was by now a beautiful sunny day, warm but not fiercely hot, with a welcome breeze moderating the temperature somewhat. I lay on some tobacco sacks I had fashioned into a perfectly adequate and comfortable sun lounger and watched the world float by. We had the river pretty much to ourselves and had seen no other vessels for a while. The regular humming of the engine was the only sound to disturb the tranquillity.

Beyond the rocks and wide beaches at the edge of the river, above steep sandy bluffs three or four metres above the water level, and presumably covered during the wet season, was a constant mass of dense verdant jungle. Occasionally, small riverside settlements on either bank broke the monotony.

From time to time, I saw ragged little children leading water buffalo down to the river. They would allow huge black, shiny beasts to drink, and wallow for a while. Fisherfolk busied themselves with their nets, harvesting the prolific waters.

At certain wide and shallow sections, the helmsman had crew members poling the river to check depths and carefully pick the best passage. The skipper needed this navigational help, but the technique was not foolproof, as we would soon find out.

Around late afternoon, there was a crunching judder and a sudden lurching halt to our forward momentum. We had grounded on a sandbank. The fast-flowing river pushed us further into the obstruction, so we were well and truly stuck.

The skipper revved the engine and thrust the gears forward and then rapidly into reverse to get us refloated, but to no avail. He had by now embedded the bow deep into the gravel and shingle.

I did not know whether this was normal for a trip down the Mekong or if I was sailing with Captain Pugwash.

We sat there midstream, unable to move. A couple of similar-sized ships came by, and I thought maybe we could have had a tow, but they did nothing to arrange this. I thought perhaps we could ring the Chinese to open up a sluice gate higher up the river or chuck some cargo overboard, but I did not know beyond that. Perhaps we would wait for the monsoons to lift us off. I went and fetched myself a beer.

From 5.30 pm, with a brief break for dinner, the skipper continued to rev the engines and throw the gears in a vain effort to release us. They brought a spectacularly bright searchlight into service to help illuminate proceedings when darkness fell. The crew called it a day at around nine, without any success.

I slept well, considering the constant percussion of a gravel-laden river smashing into a steel hull.

At 7 am the engines started up for another round of futile effort. Around 8.30, our crew engaged with a passing boat, a little smaller than ours, with a Lao family ranging from Grandma to toddlers and a saffron-robed young monk on board. They tried to persuade them to give us some help.

Reluctantly, the Laotian skipper agreed and with his help, four crew members got a line ashore. They scrambled comically up a sheer 4m high sandbank, where they hammered in a spike with a sledgehammer.

The bemused good Samaritans then continued their journey, relieved, it seemed, to do so. They did not seem to have much faith in Captain Pugwash.

The shore-based team, about a hundred metres from the rest of us, then decided that the stakes would not hold. They needed to cross the sandbank to find somewhere to get a better purchase. The plan would never work, as they had attached a heavy-duty hawser to the initial rope. There was no way the four of them could drag its weight across the sand.

I went back to my cabin to shave, and on my return, I noticed that there were only two men on the sand, seemingly just lying there asleep. The other two had disappeared. Nothing seemed to be happening. So the cook knocked up some noodles and eggs, and three or four of us had a late breakfast.

By the time I had returned to the bow from the messroom, I was astonished to see thirty-eight villagers (I counted them) ranging from young kids to fit young men, older chaps, grannies and a couple of orange-robed monks marching across the sand. A dozen or more mangy dogs were barking incessantly and excitedly at the unusual activity.

The onshore crew organised the crowd to pull the steel hawser a hundred metres or more to the edge of the sand and loop it around a hefty palm tree. I could just about make out this action in the far distance. It was a bit of a struggle, but they finally managed it.

Back onboard, powered by an auxiliary engine on the bow, they fired the windlass up. Miraculously, after a few false starts, they hauled the vessel off the sandbank. We were floating again. Within half an hour, we were ready for the off, and I resumed my default position on the tobacco sack mattress I had fashioned for a few hours in the sun. I relaxed, watching the jungle flash by on both sides. It was another warm sunny day, and after all the drama, I was happy just to read and doze.

We continued on our descent of the Mekong without further incident, and we berthed at Ban Mom border control on the Laos bank sometime mid-afternoon. I thought this was a routine customs stop where they would stamp passports, check visas, and presumably inspect the cargo. But no, I was told I was being chucked off the boat before we had reached my agreed destination.

Obviously, the lengthy delays resulting from the navigational cockups and piloting errors had forced the boat owner to rethink about getting his cargo to where it should be in time. I was just an additional problem for him. He had presumably telephoned the skipper and given his instructions.

Communication by the odd word and lots of gesticulation and shrugging clarified that I would leave the '*Ja Long Shing*' and travel on alone. After the official had checked my passport, one of the crew members rustled up a speedboat taxi man from out of nowhere. A crew member handed my hastily packed rucksack to the driver.

I tried to say they had not kept their part of the bargain and should pay for the river taxi. My heart was not really in an argument that I knew I would lose.

Oh well, c'est la vie. I had enjoyed my voyage down one of Asia's great waterways. It had all been a tremendously memorable experience, particularly the complete village coming out to our rescue. The trip had also been good value for money, particularly when I considered all the meals and beers I had consumed.

I waved goodbye to my crewmates, paid the boatman the agreed discounted rate with some of my baht, put my helmet on, and we were off at a significant speed. The vehicle was effectively a fat jet ski, not the most comfortable mode of transport, but highly exhilarating.

Amazingly fast and incredibly noisy, we shot down the river for about twenty minutes, and I would not have wanted to go much further. It was not exactly comfortable.

Whilst I had a visa to visit Laos, I had decided by now I would just settle for being dropped in Northern Thailand. I would find my way down to Chiang Mai, my second home. When we stopped at Ban Mom, the customs officials had not seemed interested in letting me into their country. The place was very remote, anyway. I thought it would be best to be pragmatic for once.

Chapter 14

A RETURN TO THAILAND AND HOME

Once formally stamped into Thailand, I quickly found the bus station and took a coach for the brief journey to Chiang Rai. I was happily navigating myself around Chiang Rai, the largest city in the country's north and one with which I was reasonably familiar.

By now, it was late afternoon, so I found Easy House, pleasant enough, centrally located, and a small hotel I had stayed at previously and secured a room. I would spend the night there and take the bus to Chiang Mai the next day.

After a bit of a wash and brush up, I headed out to have a meal and check out a couple of the live music places in town. It was good to be back in friendly, laid-back Thailand.

I took a comfortable coach late morning for the nearly two-hundred-kilometre drive to Chiang Mai. The well-maintained tarmac roads represent a significant change to what I had been experiencing in Southwest China.

I walked from the bus station to my old home, the JD Guesthouse, where Lee and Deng, who ran the place, welcomed me warmly. Brian, the ebullient Irishman, was in town and Steve, an acquaintance of earlier visits, and they told me of other comings and goings and their news. It was effortless to slip into the Chiang Mai lifestyle, and I enjoyed catching up with the gossip.

I spent a few days in Chiang Mai, revisiting favoured old haunts with the gang from JD's. These included the Pinte Blues Bar, the Saxophone Bar, the Goodview, the Riverside, Brasserie, and Night Illusion.

Lee, particularly, was a big fan of Night Illusion, while I was just okay about the place. My thinking was that the best thing about it was its late closing and closeness to home. This made it an excellent last watering hole for a night out.

The music was not to my taste but could be fun. They had a house pop band fronted by a succession of barbie dolls and good-looking boy band types, serving up constant bubble-gum songs. One night whilst we were there, a young British guy who was standing close to me jumped up on stage to sing. Right away, I could tell he had an excellent voice and stage presence.

"He's got an excellent voice," I commented to the young woman next to me, who I assumed was the singer's girlfriend.

"Yeah, he should have; he's lead singer with Toploader. He's Joe Washbourn," she drawled in a bored, dismissive rock-chick manner as if I should have known. Toploader had had a big hit with 'Dancing in the Moonlight' in 2000 and played Glastonbury, so they had some pedigree.

In the daytime, it was pleasant to wander around the narrow sois in the sunshine, check out the parks, or go for a ride on a hired bike. I visited one or two of the wats, particularly those with pleasant shady grounds, which could be very tranquil. Coffee breaks were enjoyed in agreeably quiet spots, reading the *Bangkok Post* and tackling the scrabble puzzle. It was a lazy, idyllic lifestyle.

We also used to do a bit of food shopping at the local markets. In the evenings we joined forces in the well-equipped outdoor kitchen to knock up, hopefully, authentic Thai dinners for all and sundry. When we stayed in to eat, we would drink beer and Thai whisky, listen to new CDs and chat.

However, after a few days, I found the comfortable Chiang Mai lifestyle had become a bit too familiar, and my feet itched to get on the road again. After all, my sabbatical, midlife crisis or gap year, or whatever we might term it, was ending soon.

They told me the sleeper train was fully booked for the day I wanted to go down south. So I took a coach to Phitsanulok, about halfway down to the capital and a six-hour trip - as long as I wanted to be on a coach in one hit.

Phitsanulok was a sizeable enough place, and being over 600 years old, had a significant history. It had been the provincial centre of the Khmer Empire in the distant past. For me, however, its importance derived from the fact that it conveniently broke my journey to Bangkok and was on the main railway route.

I walked from the bus terminus, a remote soulless spot a mile or two out of town, and readily found the train station. Accommodation for the night was my next requirement so that I could stay somewhere convenient for my onward travels. Immediately opposite was a sad and rundown commercial hotel, but it offered adequate facilities at a budget rate. It would be fine.

I went through the formalities with the Chinese owner, dropped my bag off in my room, and went out to explore. I strolled down to where I could see a bridge over the River Nan, which was a broad and sizeable watercourse, in the middle distance.

To the left, before I had reached the bridge, I saw a sign for the night market and decided I would go down and have a look. It was by now late afternoon. As I turned the corner, a fleet of bicycle rickshaws transported a crowd of about twenty western tourists on some sort of organised tour. Five minutes later, I caught up with them as they were being herded into an outdoor 'flying vegetable' restaurant on the riverside.

This was a phenomenon that the city traded on that they had invented all of ten or fifteen years earlier as a tourist attraction. I stopped as I was a little intrigued and ordered a beer, taking a seat where I had a grandstand view of the proceedings.

Essentially, the flying vegetable show comprised a chef frying morning glory and other mixed vegetables in a wok, with flames everywhere. He would then nonchalantly and theatrically slinging the contents over his shoulder to where an eagle-eyed waiter deftly caught the lot on his plate. (I keep referring to this sort of episode, but what restaurants in SE Asia could get away with was so far removed from our rigorously controlled regimes back home. Our Health and Safety fraternity in the UK would be highly unlikely to approve of such shenanigans.)

They then repeated the process, and to spice things up a bit, browbeat a volunteer to take part in the show. They would leave the safety of the crowd of shrieking tourists and clamber up a ladder onto the roof of a minibus. The poor unfortunate then had to go through a practice run with the server showing her (in the case I saw) the ropes. Then she was on her own, and to great acclaim, pulled the trick off successfully. Vegetables were all caught. It was all slightly bizarre.

I finished my beer and walked on down the waterfront to find somewhere a bit more traditional for my evening meal.

After eating some standard fare, I meandered back, looping through the night market, which was gradually closing down by this stage. Scores of traders were selling vegetables they had laid out on a cloth on the pavement. Others had stopped trading and had curled up by their pitches to sleep for the night. It was a Friday, so I didn't know whether this was a weekend occurrence or these people literally worked, lived and slept on the pavement daily. Whichever the case, it was a shockingly harsh existence.

In the morning, I crossed the road to catch my Bangkok train. It was due to leave at 10.10 am but according to the stationmaster, would not be leaving until 11.10 am and only offered third-class accommodation, which did not sound great.

As I now had some time to kill, I left my rucksack with the obliging hotel owner and looked around town a little more. It surprised me to see that it was now all changed at the riverside with the disappearance of several of the pop-up flying vegetable restaurants. Serried ranks of dozens of men and women had replaced them. They were sitting in front of treadle-operated sewing machines, beavering away repairing or making clothing. There were also scores of individual traders selling and repairing jewellery.

A careful examination of the area revealed some substantial lockable steel cabinets. These presumably contained equipment that would they again would bring into play for the evening vegetable throwing sessions.

I walked on, avoiding the manic tuk-tuk drivers who were out in force, and circled back to the station, where I found two trains were waiting to depart. The one I had booked was supposed to be the quickest but had only basic accommodation and no restaurant car, but I decided not to change. Maybe, on reflection, not the best decision.

Initially, everything was okay with the sun still to reach its zenith and the train not being too busy. I was sitting opposite a quite sizeable young German man, and both of us had spread out over two designated seats on the hard wooden benches.

However, within an hour, the sun was blazing down fiercely and unforgivingly, and the train had become very busy. To make matters worse, the ancient oscillating fan above us had packed up.

As we were both now wholly jammed into our seats by fellow passengers, I exchanged glances with the German. We had an unspoken understanding that we were going through hell, but that there was not a lot we could do about it. Our limbs were wedged so tightly, it was not possible to scratch an itch or suppress a sneeze, and I could feel rivulets of sweat trickling all down my body.

Major engineering works slowed our progress, and we waited for ages at tiny little rural stations. There was constant dust from the extensive operations on the track. Then, to make matters infinitely worse, we found we were travelling through an extensive grain-producing area and that it was the stubble-burning time of year. Thick acrid smoke from the fields came in through the open windows. Any countryside visible was flat and featureless.

Of course, the projected six-and-a-half-hour journey had by now extended to seven-and-a-half. The last hour was dreadful, being painfully slow with frequent stops at every suburban station on the line and a lengthy hiatus at Bangkok airport.

I had tried to remain calm on the journey, withdrawing into my little daydream world to ease the situation. Particularly in the stubble-burning section. Once into the greater Bangkok area, there was more to see out of the windows, which helped pass the time.

In between the many railway lines and shunting tracks, toddlers were amusing themselves. Older children played games or flew kites with adults, and scores of street dogs just ambled around doing what dogs do. Women sat on railway lines nursing babies, chatting with their friends or busying themselves with embroidery. It was pretty incongruous seeing all this day-to-day life carrying on as usual in the middle of a primary railway system in a vast sprawling metropolis. In some places, there were full-scale markets set up on sparse pockets of land between the rails.

Pitifully shabby shacks constructed out of pieces of discarded corrugated iron or plastic sheeting at the side of the tracks were home to these people. Filthy-looking khongs or canals were the water source for washing clothes and themselves. Hopefully, they did not use these for drinking water.

We finally pulled into Hualamphong station, and I felt quite a relief to have finally reached Bangkok. My German friend smiled at me to show the same emotion as we all disappeared into the crowds of people and traffic madness of Thailand's capital.

I needed to get to somewhere where I could get a shower and a change of clothes quickly. There was a quirky place called the Atlanta hotel on Sukhumvit, which I had read about somewhere. I would give it a whirl and give the Khao San Road a miss this time.

Taking a motorbike taxi for the quick journey, the driver dropped me at the entrance to Soi 2 off the main Sukhumvit Road.

According to *Lonely Planet*, the Atlanta was 'an historic hotel owned since its construction by Dr Max Henn. The good Doctor was a former secretary to the Maharaja of Bikaner and sometime Indochina agent'. It further said that the hostelry offered clean and acceptable rooms at a reasonable rate and had a leafy garden, a swimming pool and a classical 50s-style lobby.

I found it, just a couple of hundred metres off the busy main road. Amazingly, it was in a very peaceful area with plenty of mature leafy trees full of twittering birds. However, it looked more than dated, it was an anachronism.

The owner, an idiosyncratic old German, did not offer an enthusiastic welcome, in fact, no welcome at all. He just glared at me, and with a dismissive arm, directed me to a receptionist. He had obviously personally trained this woman in the art of autocratic, charmless and indifferent hotel management.

After much sighing, huffing and harrumphing, they deigned to let me have a room. I filled out a lengthy form confirming that I agreed to the lengthy list of things guests could not do whilst in the hotel, and then the receptionist barked,

"Passport!"

Basil Fawlty would not have had a look in here.

She barked the ultimate words after giving me a room key,

"Read the notices, please."

At least, I think she said please.

On the wall of the lobby were many notices instructing inmates on such matters as what to wear, when the hotel closed, and what time we should vacate rooms. There were also injunctions not to ask for more towels or shampoo sachets.

One sign highlighted the hotel's music policy and programme. The programme specified:

12-1 pm Music composed by the King.

1-5 pm Big Band Music.

Evenings Classical Jazz.

At the bottom of the poster was 'Definitely (underlined) No Pop Music.'

Another sign said guests could not bring catamites to the room. I had to check that one out, not being familiar with the term. It would not be an issue as it disallowed the bringing in of young boys for homosexual purposes.

The last sign simply said, 'The Management will not tolerate complaints.'

Obviously, I had some second thoughts about the place after experiencing this approach, but after the journey I had had, I was determined to see it through.

I paid three times my Chiang Mai rate - and they had my money without me even seeing the room; I was also told I had to share a bathroom rather than the private facilities I thought I had negotiated.

No chance.

They then sent over an ex-Gestapo officer at a desk in the corner who would escort me to my cell.

I carried my rucksack up to the room, which the chap opened. The general factotum then switched the fan on and stood back, hovering for a tip. I let him hover. After a bit of a standoff, he made a derogatory guttural noise and finally left with no pecuniary benefit.

The room itself was fine, and as I only shared the bathroom with the room next door, it was all alright. Right away, I made use of the powerful shower to wash off the grime and sweat of the horrendous journey. Then twenty minutes later, dressed in fresh clothes, I was ready for an evening in Bangkok.

I had booked the Atlanta for three nights, but really Bangkok was just a staging post while I decided what to do for my final two weeks. As I had an unused visa, I could go up and see more of Laos. However, I favoured the idea of some R&R on Ko Samet, probably the nearest relatively unspoiled Thai island. I wanted to enjoy some relaxing beach time, and to make sure that I went home with a decent tan.

Having walked up and down the busy thronging Sukhumvit Road and immersed myself in the sights, sounds and aromas of downtown Bangkok, I found a quieter, sophisticated little restaurant just off the main drag. I enjoyed a pleasant and relaxing traditional Thai meal.

Over an apéritif, I confirmed in my mind that I would go to Ko Samet. An enjoyable few days of idyllic island life before heading back to the English spring would go down well.

I had been on the road for the best part of a year by now. It had been an epic adventure, and I had enjoyed so many experiences and meeting such a diverse range of people. I had kept in touch by new-fangled (for me) email and the odd phone call. But it would be good to catch up with friends and family once more in the flesh.

Soon I would have to think about where I would live when I got back to Blighty and how I would make a living - trifling matters like that. But those considerations could wait a while.

After a period of reflection and contemplation over my meal and having decided upon a plan of action, I threw myself into the Bangkok nightlife. I found a couple of live rock venues over the next couple of hours before returning to Atlanta with absolutely no catamites in tow.

I relaxed over a coffee in Atlanta's beautiful tropical gardens in the morning and sat overlooking the pool. The place was growing on me. If I ignored the staff as far as possible, I could enjoy my time at this dated, idiosyncratic hotel, which I was discovering was not without a certain charm.

I appreciated not rushing off anywhere and, as no other guests were to be seen, enjoyed the peace and tranquillity on my own for an hour or two.

Over the next couple of days, at a modest pace, I checked out more of Bangkok. This exploration included visiting a couple of riverside wats, taking longtail boat rides down the Chao Phraya, and finding Jim Thompson's house.

(Thompson was the American entrepreneur who kick-started the Thai silk industry and then mysteriously disappeared without a trace in 1967 in the Cameron Highlands in Malaysia.)

 I also wandered around various parks, markets, and previously unexplored districts and took the overhead monorail for a different view of the city.

Other time I spent around, and indeed in, the quiet pool at the Atlanta, while in the evenings finding bars and restaurants was pretty easy given my prime location.

After my third night, I finally left the Atlanta hotel, took a motorbike taxi out to the bus station. I caught a coach to Rayong and then a local bus east a few kilometres to Ban Phe. This fishing village was also the ferry port for Ko Samet. The island was an hour further on from tacky and tawdry Pattaya; but a world away in style and class.

It was idyllic with tourist brochure white sand beaches fringed with rocky headlands and lapped by warm aquamarine waters. A little more developed than Ko Lanta, but less so than many other islands, the place was ideal for a few days' beach holiday.

The accommodation was in one of the ubiquitous little huts with a bathroom, a large double bed and a porch complete with a hammock and sea view. For three or four quid a night, I couldn't complain.

They required me to pay the equivalent of a few pounds on entry to the island. However, as this was a 'National Park Fee', I did not begrudge this. I sincerely hoped they would spend it wisely on maintaining biodiversity and managing and minimising the impact of tourism. As with other Thai islands, water supply, refuse disposal, and sewage treatment remained sizeable issues.

I spent a pleasant few days enjoying the beach and the sea, walking some trails and having a relaxed time in the sunshine. I met up with a few other travellers in the evenings for drinks, chats, and meals. It was all most convivial.

After a few days, though, I had had enough of the beach scene, and an email from Chiang Mai prompted me to return to Thailand's northern capital. The gang were looking forward to celebrating Songkran. This is the most important festival in the Thai year and a critical date in the Buddhist calendar, as it is their New Year. They told me Chiang Mai was the best place to celebrate and I should visit one last time before heading back home.

In three or four hours, I got up to Bangkok and then hacked across the city in absolutely sweltering heat on a motorbike taxi. With the temperature, the traffic fumes and a heavy backpack, it was not a pleasant experience. At traffic lights, which seem to be red for ages, all the many dozens of motorbikes came to the front of the queue, beyond the four-wheeled vehicles and tuk-tuks. We then spent the five or seven minutes it took for the lights to change, revving and spewing out toxic fumes in the 40-degree heat. It wasn't great.

On the sleeper, my trip up to Chiang Mai was infinitely more enjoyable than my third class, hard bench experience a week earlier. A couple of beers, some Thai whisky, a pleasant meal in the restaurant car and a chat with some fellow travellers was the order of the evening. It was then a matter of getting my head down in a comfortable bunk - that was the way to travel.

Back at the JD Guesthouse, there was growing excitement about Songkran coming up at the weekend. The actual date of the festival is the 13th of April. However, as the Thais enjoyed a party, the festival seemed to extend a few days on either side of this date.

It was a week of celebrations, as the day I got back to my northern Thai home was my birthday. Any excuse meant a meal out at the Goodview with Lee and Deng and a motley crew of travellers who were hanging out at JD's. It also, as oft before, finished up at Night Illusion for a bit of a late session with the obligatory Thai whisky and some bopping to the pop bands.

The locals saw Thursday as a Songkran warmup day, with people out in their thousands in the town centre getting into the swing of things.

A small posse from JD's made the short walk into town to see what all the fuss was all about.

The celebration is essentially a water festival and comprises people drenching other people all day. Buckets of water, sponges, water pistols, or firing, as was increasingly popular, the large, high-powered, plastic, pump-action water guns was the modus operandi. It seemed anything went, and it was (essentially) all taken in good spirits.

A perimeter of small canals, which provided an inexhaustible water supply for the combatants, conveniently surrounded the old city. Before Songkran, the authorities had cleaned the canals out and topped up the levels to ensure that dousing would be with reasonably clean water. Not the murky, slimy stuff that usually stagnated there.

I had read calls in the *Bangkok Post* for restraint in celebrating the festival, primarily because of the endless possibilities for accidents and incidents. However, the Thai character does not do restraint. Soberly, the article pointed out that Chiang Mai topped the league for accidents in the previous year, with 540 registered over the holiday period.

Everyone seemed soaked through; people drove pickup trucks with half-naked young men in the back around the streets with forty-gallon drums of water from which to refill their monster water guns. Some of these drums had large blocks of ice in them. With the air temperature in the high thirties, a soaking in ambient temperatures was quite acceptable, but the ice-cold water was something else. Being drenched with freezing water was a heart-stopping shock to the system.

Scores of people were filling buckets from the moats to give the pickup-riding boys something to think about, so it became quite a battle. There were also some basic water vending machines strategically placed to keep people supplied.

There was an authentic carnival atmosphere already. Although some stalls and sideshows were still under construction, plenty of traders were selling souvenirs, grilled snacks and drinks. Some places were pumping out loud Thai pop.

As well as pickup trucks, the ubiquitous motorbikes were cruising around the block with, again, mainly young men with three or even four on board. All were all armed with water cannons to drench the crowds.

I slipped away from the action for a while to get some running repairs carried out on my sandals, sleeping bag, and my rucksack. Finding skilled and inexpensive tailors and shoe repairers was very easy in Chiang Mai.

Thursday night, we partied hard and followed this up with a full day's water fighting in the hot sunshine on Friday.

Songkran, I also learned, was also a time for meeting up with family, exchanging presents and paying respects to elderly relatives. The older people restricted the water element in the festival, to sprinkling perfumed water from a tiny silver bowl whilst wishing everyone a happy new year. Most of these muted celebrations wisely took place away from the city centre and the canals. Here, the younger elements demonstrated more exuberant behaviour.

Back in the heart of the action, besides water being thrown everywhere, the crowds also brought coloured powder paints and flour into play, making the streets an absolute mess.

On Friday, after the water-based activities for the day, we bought food at the night market for a change. We had a convivial evening back at base, with everyone helping with the preparations and the cooking as a prelude to a more mellow evening.

Saturday was my last day in Chiang Mai before taking the overnight train down to Bangkok and flying home the following evening. So, while I enjoyed everything and entered the spirit of the occasion, I was feeling a little more reflective about my year away from the UK and what the future held for me.

I was confident I would be okay, being, by nature, an optimist. I felt I had sufficient skills and experience to make a living and find a decent place to live now that the marital home was no longer. So I determined I would go back to the UK in a positive frame of mind, ready to face any challenges thrown at me.

Late afternoon as the sun slipped below the 1676m peak, I found myself alone in a quiet bar with a beautiful view of the majestic Doi Suthep some 15km to the west of the city. I was in a contemplative mood.

I felt at home in Thailand, particularly in this beautiful northern outpost, and I believed I had learned something valuable from the Buddhist religion. The Buddhist way of life is about positive thoughts and actions, love, kindness, and wisdom. Problems arise from confused and negative states of mind, and there is a need to overcome anger, jealousy and ignorance and develop compassion. I could happily embrace this philosophy.

I sipped my beer and promised myself that whatever happened in the future, travel was going to be a top priority. A return to Chiang Mai would have to be on the cards.

Later that evening, I made my final and emotional goodbyes to the JD crew and headed to the station.

Arriving in Bangkok early the following day, I had the whole day until late evening before flying home. Dropping my rucksack off at the left luggage room at the station, I had some breakfast at a pavement café close to the station.

After a leisurely couple of cups of coffee, I did some further exploration. I thought Songkran had peaked, or indeed was over, but it was still in full swing in the capital. Again, bare-chested lads in pickup trucks were racing around the streets, firing the monster water guns and flinging flour and paint everywhere. Keen to avoid a soaking, I took a ferry across the river to a quieter area of the city.

I walked around some pleasant leafy sois with minimal traffic on that Sunday morning and enjoyed hearing birdsong, a bit of a rarity in mega-busy Bangkok. An enjoyable hour later, I took a break at a charming little café near Wat Arun, the Temple of Dawn, and picked up a *Bangkok Post*.

Unsurprisingly, the headlines on the front page made grim reading. There had been two hundred seventy-nine people fatalities to date during the Songkran Festival, with over 20,000 injured. Most casualties were among the young lads.

Over the river, I saw scores of them on the broad avenues powering down the road on motorbikes with their exhaust systems disconnected to maximise the noise. Wearing just shorts, they drove speedily and recklessly. Their passengers held large water cannons in both hands and stood barefoot on the stirrups as they sought prospective victims. Hazardous vehicle-to-vehicle water fights also took place. The authorities certainly need to take action to prevent such a pointless waste of young lives.

*

I later took a longtail boat trip up and down the river, which was always a great way to see the city., Afterwards, I wandered back to the busy and vibrant area around the station, where I stayed until my train was due.

I had a lengthy meal at a relatively upmarket little restaurant and enjoyed a last couple of Chang beers before heading out to the airport.

After a long overnight flight, I emerged from the Heathrow terminal into the fresh spring sunshine.

On arriving back at my home station a couple of hours later, I walked the twenty minutes to my daughter's house, where I would stay for a while. I found it all so evocative. That mid-April morning, in the bright sunshine, England was looking at its best. A green and pleasant land indeed, with the daffodils in full bloom. The sound of lawnmowers in the background and the earthy perfume of new-mown grass in the air.

It was good to be back home after such incredible adventures. I would plan more.